Regional Responses to U.S.-China Competition in the Indo-Pacific

Japan

Scott W. Harold

Prepared for the United States Air Force
Approved for public release; distribution unlimited

RAND PROJECT AIR FORCE

For more information on this publication, visit www.rand.org/t/RR4412z4

For more information on this series, visit www.rand.org/US-PRC-influence

Library of Congress Cataloging-in-Publication Data is available for this publication.

ISBN: 978-1-9774-0519-7

Published by the RAND Corporation, Santa Monica, Calif.

© Copyright 2020 RAND Corporation

RAND® is a registered trademark.

Cover: globe: jcrosemann/GettyImages; flags: luzitanija/Adobe Stock

www.rand.org

Preface

The 2017 U.S. National Security Strategy and the National Defense Strategy summary describe a world characterized by a return to great-power competition, most notably with China in the Indo-Pacific region. U.S. allies and partners will play a crucial role in ensuring outcomes to that competition that favor freedom, democracy, and a security order in which the interests and values represented by the rules-based international order remain strong. America's enduring alliance with Japan not only is the cornerstone of U.S. force posture in the Indo-Pacific region, but also magnifies and bolsters U.S. influence across that vast swath of territory. Within the region, Southeast Asian countries have been particularly exposed to China's expanding influence and coercive diplomacy in recent years, making the ten countries of the Association of Southeast Asian Nations a key focus for U.S. national strategy and the U.S. Department of Defense (DoD) in particular. This study focuses on how best to leverage the U.S.-Japan alliance to engage in a long-term strategic competition with China in the Southeast Asia region, at least out to 2030.

This report on the U.S.–Japan alliance and Southeast Asia is part of a broader project that aims to understand the perspectives of U.S. allies and partners in the Indo-Pacific as they formulate and implement their responses to China's more assertive foreign and security policy behavior in the region and a more competitive U.S.-China relationship. The research also assesses how DoD, particularly the U.S. Air Force, can best deepen and improve its ability to work with Japan to ensure that Southeast Asian nations have options other than simply bandwagoning with or submitting to Chinese dominance. The other reports in this series are available at www.rand.org/US-PRC-influence.

The research reported here was sponsored by Brig Gen Michael P. Winkler (PACAF/A5/8) and conducted within the Strategy and Doctrine Program of RAND Project AIR FORCE as part of a fiscal year 2019 project titled "Regional Responses to U.S.-China Competition in the Indo-Pacific" that assists the Air Force in evaluating U.S. and Chinese influence and assessing possible Air Force, joint force, and U.S. government options. Research was completed in September 2019.

RAND Project AIR FORCE

RAND Project AIR FORCE (PAF), a division of the RAND Corporation, is the Department of the Air Force's (DAF's) federally funded research and development center for studies and analyses. PAF provides the DAF with independent analyses of policy alternatives affecting the development, employment, combat readiness, and support of current and future air, space, and cyber forces. Research is conducted in four programs: Strategy and Doctrine, Force

Modernization and Employment; Manpower, Personnel, and Training; and Resource Management. The research reported here was prepared under contract FA7014-16-D-1000.

Additional information about PAF is available on our website: www.rand.org/paf/

This report documents work originally shared with the Department of the Air Force on September 26, 2019. The draft report, issued on March 20, 2020, was reviewed by formal peer reviewers and DAF subject-matter experts.

Contents

Figures

Tables

Summary

Issue

This report is part of a broader project that aims to understand the roles of U.S. allies and partners in the Indo-Pacific in strategic competition with China and to assess how the U.S. Department of Defense (DoD) and, more specifically, the U.S. Air Force (USAF) can best deepen and improve their ability to work with these allies and partners to maintain U.S. advantage in long-term strategic competition with China. In this report, the author assesses the prospects for deepening U.S.-Japan alliance cooperation and coordination in Southeast Asia to compete with China in that subregion of the Indo-Pacific, posing two key analytical questions:

1. To what extent is Japan open to broader and deeper cooperation and coordination with the United States to compete with China in Southeast Asia?
2. To the extent that Japan is open to working with the United States to counter Chinese influence in the Southeast Asian region, what possible steps could the allies take to deepen cooperation and more effectively counter China's ambitions there?

Approach

To explore the answers to these questions, the author surveyed official Japanese documents, drew on a wide variety of secondary source analyses, and conducted face-to-face interviews with approximately 25 Japanese defense and foreign policy officials, military officers, think-tank analysts, and academic specialists under promise of anonymity.

Main Findings

Although Japan has long engaged with Southeast Asia on diplomatic, economic, and security ties, it has expanded the scope of its diplomatic and defense engagements with regional counterparts in recent years in an effort to bolster and preserve the rules-based international order that it sees China as threatening. Japan has used security cooperation and assistance to empower Southeast Asian nations to resist Chinese coercion, creating opportunities for the United States to work with Japan and Southeast Asia in new ways, both operationally and diplomatically.

Recommendations

The U.S. government should consider the following recommendations with respect to strengthening defense and security cooperation with Japan in the Southeast Asian region:

- **Leveraging the U.S.-Japan alliance in the strategic competition with China in Southeast Asia requires "winning the peace."** Southeast Asian nations will not contribute much (if anything) in an actual conflict with China under most contingencies, so competition with China in Southeast Asia will mainly center on the contest for influence during peacetime, meaning a focus on norms-setting, access agreements, and building up closer diplomatic ties that shape outcomes in which the United States and Japan achieve their preferred outcomes without having to fight an armed conflict against China.

- **Security cooperation with Japan is favorably viewed by most in Southeast Asia (see Figure S.1), making it attractive to the United States to jointly articulate a policy framework of defense engagement with Japan built around support for Association of Southeast Asian Nations (ASEAN) centrality and the values of autonomy, capacity, and resiliency.** The United States and Japan could jointly host a summit with ASEAN at which they articulate their principles for deepening engagement with Southeast Asian nations across a variety of security ties.

Figure S.1. Strong Support for Expanding Japan-ASEAN Security Cooperation

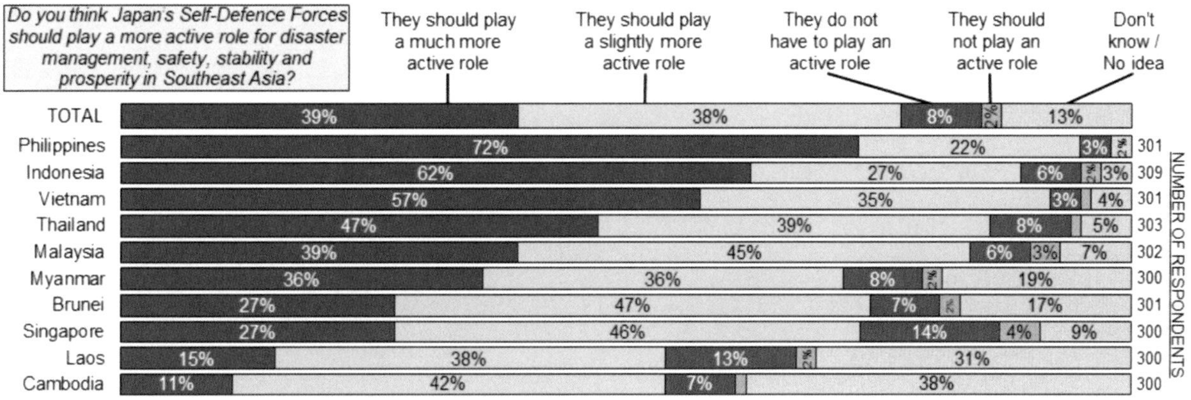

SOURCE: Ministry of Foreign Affairs of Japan, 2017b.

DoD and the USAF should consider the following recommendation to leverage the U.S.-Japan alliance to compete with China in Southeast Asia:

- **Because ASEAN nations seek to avoid appearing to be drawn into an anti-China coalition, strive to frame U.S.-Japan security cooperation in Southeast Asia, wherever possible, around assistance designed to support norms and deal with transnational threats that require capabilities that would also be useful in the event of a contingency with China.** Ensure that plans and programs to engage Southeast Asian nations are coordinated, deconflicted, and designed to achieve synergy with Japanese efforts insofar as this is possible. Consider engaging with Japan in planning and exercising humanitarian assistance and disaster relief operations focused on responding to a crisis in Southeast Asia. Expanding professional military education opportunities for Southeast Asian nations in the United States and Japan is another worthwhile avenue to invest in. Explore opportunities to work with Japan to shape regional militaries through assistance programs focused on building partner air and maritime domain capacity, cyber defense, and critical infrastructure protection. Leverage Japan's expertise on logistics, maintenance, and training and exercises, and look for opportunities to trilateralize training and exercises with regional allies and partners in Southeast Asia so that they get used to operating in tandem with U.S. and Japanese forces. Use information-sharing together with exchanges focused on the international laws and regulations governing air and maritime spaces to publicly highlight China's problematic behavior in the South China Sea and elsewhere and the rights ASEAN states enjoy, as well as their policy options.

Acknowledgments

The author wishes to thank the numerous current and former Japanese and U.S. government officials, members of the Self-Defense Forces and the U.S. Air Force, think-tank analysts in Japan and the United States, and Japanese academics and foreign affairs–oriented journalists who gave generously of their schedules and shared their insights during the course of the project. The author is also grateful to Paula Thornhill, Raphael Cohen, Bonny Lin, Michael S. Chase, Jennifer D. P. Moroney, Jeffrey W. Hornung, and Eric Larson of RAND and Jim Schoff of the Carnegie Endowment for International Peace for guidance and helpful reviews of draft versions of the report.

Abbreviations

A2/AD	anti-access/area denial
ADIZ	Air Defense Identification Zone
ASEAN	Association of Southeast Asian Nations
C4ISR	command, control, communications, computers, intelligence, surveillance, and reconnaissance
CDP	Constitutional Democratic Party
CSD	collective self-defense
DoD	U.S. Department of Defense
DPFP	Democratic Party for the People
DPJ	Democratic Party of Japan
FOIP	Free and Open Indo-Pacific
HA/DR	humanitarian assistance and disaster relief
ISR	intelligence, surveillance, and reconnaissance
JASDF	Japan Air Self-Defense Force
JCP	Japan Communist Party
JGSDF	Japan Ground Self-Defense Force
JMSDF	Japan Maritime Self-Defense Force
LDP	Liberal Democratic Party
NDPG	National Defense Program Guidelines
PLA	People's Liberation Army
PRC	People's Republic of China
SDF	Self-Defense Forces (Japan)
UN	United Nations
UNSC	United Nations Security Council
USAF	U.S. Air Force

1. The U.S.-Japan Alliance, Southeast Asia, and China's Rise

The 2017 U.S. National Security Strategy and the National Defense Strategy summary describe a world characterized by the return of great power competition, most notably in the Indo-Pacific region with the People's Republic of China (PRC). U.S. allies and partners will play a crucial role in ensuring outcomes to that competition that favor freedom, democracy, and a security order in which the interests and values represented by the rules-based international order remain strong. As numerous recent studies by leading U.S. analysts specializing in Asia have recognized, America's enduring alliance with Japan is the cornerstone of U.S. force posture and influence in the Indo-Pacific region and is especially important for competition with China.[1] Within the region, Southeast Asian countries have been particularly exposed to China's expanding influence and coercive diplomacy in recent years, making the ten countries of the Association of Southeast Asian Nations (ASEAN) (in particular, key U.S. allies the Philippines and Thailand) an important focus for U.S. national strategy and for the U.S. Department of Defense (DoD) in particular. As one leading U.S. subject-matter expert argues, Southeast Asia could play a role as a "harbinger," contending that "as goes Southeast Asia, so goes the international order."[2] Separately, a recent report published by the Center for a New American Security identifies Southeast Asia as "the most contested region in the Indo-Pacific," where "the United States and its allies—above all, Japan—are engaged in a competition with China to shape the development and governance pathways of countries in the region, as well as their overall strategic alignments."[3] Although there are arguably many important regional and functional areas that the United States and Japan could focus on in striving to better compete with China, this report focuses specifically on the question of how the United States can best leverage its alliance with Japan to compete with China in Southeast Asia and identifies the elements of a competitive strategy that the region would respond favorably to.[4]

---

[1] Robert D. Blackwill and Ashley J. Tellis, *Revising U.S. Grand Strategy Toward China*, Washington, D.C.: Council on Foreign Relations Special Report No. 72, March 2015; Dennis C. Blair, *Assertive Engagement: An Updated U.S.-Japan Strategy for China*, Washington, D.C.: Sasakawa Peace Foundation, 2016; Kurt M. Campbell, *The Pivot: The Future of American Statecraft in Asia*, New York: Twelve, 2016; Michael J. Green, *By More Than Providence: Grand Strategy and American Power in the Asia Pacific Since 1783*, New York: Columbia University Press, 2017; Richard L. Armitage and Joseph P. Nye, *More Important Than Ever: Renewing the U.S.-Japan Alliance for the 21st Century*, Washington, D.C.: Center for Strategic and International Studies, October 2018.

[2] Author interview with U.S. think-tank expert, Washington, D.C., March 2019.

[3] Patrick M. Cronin, Abigail Grace, Daniel Kliman, and Kristine Lee, *Contested Spaces: A Renewed Approach to Southeast Asia*, Washington, D.C.: Center for a New American Security, March 2019, p. 3.

[4] This report does not take a position on whether Southeast Asia is the most important area in which to focus the energies of the U.S.-Japan alliance in competing with China. The author merely describes what a competitive strategy toward that region that seeks to leverage the alliance might look like.

The question of how best to leverage the U.S.-Japan alliance to engage in a long-term strategic competition with China in the Southeast Asia region is the focus of this report, which is part of a broader effort that aims to understand the perspectives of U.S. allies and partners in the Indo-Pacific as they respond to China's more assertive foreign and security policy behavior in the region and to a more competitive U.S.-China relationship. The author assesses how DoD and, in particular, the U.S. Air Force (USAF) can best deepen and improve their ability to work with Japan to ensure that Southeast Asian nations have options other than simply bandwagoning with China or submitting to PRC dominance. Although some of the steps described in this report might appear to be short-term efforts, these short-term efforts can have long-term payoffs that will make things increasingly difficult for China to leverage its size, location, and capabilities to coerce the region, thereby contributing to winning the long-term strategic competition with the PRC.[5]

Drawing on a review of official Japanese government documents, secondary source materials, open-source media reporting, trade data and public opinion polls, and interviews with more than 40 officials and experts in Japan and the United States, the author explores how the United States and Japan see Southeast Asia and the prospects for working more closely with Japan in the defense realm to compete with China in that critical region. He concludes that, as one interviewee argued, the U.S.-Japan alliance can be helpful in two key roles. First, the alliance can present an additional challenge that complicates China's regional calculus, forcing it to contend not only with the influence and capabilities of the United States, but also with that of Japan. Second, Japan can act as a "wingman" for the United States in the region, helping facilitate continued U.S. access and relations across the region by providing politically desirable top cover for Southeast Asian nations to engage with the United States by framing this engagement in a context that is not binary (i.e., the United States or China) but rather is multilateral and therefore more legitimate in regional eyes.[6] The alliance can thus augment the inherent strengths of the United States as a distant power with attractive soft power and trade and investment ties with Southeast Asia. Together with the United States, Japan can provide a wide variety of intelligence and logistics support, as well as military training and capabilities development assistance to regional partners. Japan can help the United States compete with China in Southeast Asia by complementing the U.S. focus on military hard power with additional security soft power assistance in the form of institutional capacity-building, maritime law enforcement aid, dual-use infrastructure development, training and exercise opportunities, professional military education, and humanitarian assistance and disaster relief (HA/DR).

Japan can also help offset Chinese influence with countries where the U.S. relationship is relatively weak or undergoing stress. For example, when U.S. ties with Thailand experienced a decline as a consequence of that country's 2014 coup d'état, Japan was able to continue engaging

---

[5] The author thanks his colleague Jeffrey W. Hornung for suggesting he clarify this point.

[6] Author interview with Japanese government official, Tokyo, April 2019.

2

the leadership of General Prayuth Chan-o-cha. Similarly, when President Rodrigo Duterte of the Philippines began engaging in widespread human rights abuses as part of a purported war on drugs, Tokyo was able to engage Manila at times when Washington's influence was on the wane. For these reasons, RAND researchers in a 2019 study argued that alliances play a critical role in extending U.S. power and influence.[7]

Through its engagement with Southeast Asian partners, Japan can also help undercut Chinese efforts to portray the United States as an outsider meddling in Asian affairs by making clear that Tokyo welcomes U.S. involvement in regional forums and believes other countries should too. A fully engaged U.S.-Japan alliance additionally serves to undercut attempts by Beijing to frame the issue of regional competition as a great-power contest, instead reframing the questions the region faces as a choice between a broadly supported "free and open Indo-Pacific" approach that works for everyone as long as they play by the same set of rules and a hierarchical, Chinese-dominated order in which might makes right.[8]

In more-specific areas, the U.S.-Japan alliance, if properly engaged, can present Southeast Asian nations—including those that are already U.S. allies as well as those that are budding partners or even on the fence or leaning toward China—with greater options for foreign policy orientation than simply acquiescing to Chinese hegemony. By providing Southeast Asian countries with opportunities to engage on issues that matter to them—building capacity and resiliency so as to reinforce autonomy—the U.S.-Japan alliance can help prevent countries from feeling like they have no choice but to accept Chinese aid and submit to what China demands of them.

The key for leveraging the alliance, however, is that it should not be presented to Southeast Asian nations as a stark choice between the U.S.-Japan alliance and China. The goal for Washington and Tokyo should be to reinforce ASEAN unity and centrality and make China be the one that forces choices, since this will be resented by any Southeast Asian nation that is forced in this way. The U.S.-Japan alliance should engage Southeast Asian allies, partners, and interlocutors from a framework that emphasizes respect for their autonomy and seeks to bolster that autonomy by building up Southeast Asian nations' military and security capacity in selected areas, as well as reinforcing their resiliency to coercion and natural or man-made disasters.

Because many Southeast Asian nations continue to engage in egregious human rights violations, and since mutual trust within ASEAN remains a challenge, most of the defense and security assistance that the U.S.-Japan alliance offers to Southeast Asia will necessarily be in the

---

[7] Scott W. Harold, Derek Grossman, Brian Harding, Jeffrey W. Hornung, Greg Poling, Jeffrey Smith, and Meagan L. Smith, *The Thickening Web of Asian Security Cooperation: Deepening Defense Ties Among U.S. Allies and Partners in the Indo-Pacific*, Santa Monica, Calif.: RAND Corporation, RR-3125-MCF, 2019.

[8] U.S. Department of State Office of the Spokesperson, "Advancing a Free and Open Indo-Pacific Region," November 18, 2018; DoD, *Indo-Pacific Strategy Report: Preparedness, Partnerships, and Promoting a Networked Region*, Washington, D.C., June 1, 2019.

areas of nonlethal capabilities that are unlikely to be used for domestic repression.[9] Promising areas for expanding U.S.-Japan security cooperation with Southeast Asian partners include: intelligence, surveillance, and reconnaissance (ISR) and information fusion, processing, sharing, and distribution, especially for air domain awareness and maritime domain awareness; military training and exercises, including training in international law; facilities construction, maintenance, and repair; logistics; humanitarian assistance and disaster relief; cyber hygiene and network resiliency assistance; and visit, board, search, and seizure training for regional navies and maritime law enforcement forces.

Organization of the Report

The remainder of the study unfolds as follows.

In Chapter 2, the author lays out the importance of understanding Japan's domestic political landscape for assessing its willingness to compete with China in Southeast Asia, taking note of the role of political party competition, public opinion, and major economic interests (such as the business sector, tourism, or academia) that might serve as a check on Japanese willingness to help the United States compete with China in Southeast Asia.

In Chapter 3, the author advances the analysis further, drilling down on the evolution of Japan's foreign and national security policies and policymaking in light of the threat Tokyo perceives from China, thereby setting a baseline for understanding how willing Japan might be to aid the United States in competing with China in Southeast Asia.

In Chapter 4, the author describes Japan's defense and security cooperation with Southeast Asian nations to date, highlighting areas where the ground has already been prepared and where allied cooperation might be expanded further.

Finally, in Chapter 5, the author provides an overall outlook on the prospects for U.S.-Japan defense and security cooperation in Southeast Asia over the next ten years (to 2030), potential signposts for how to know the direction in which matters are developing, and a set of recommendations for U.S. defense policymakers and the USAF.

---

[9] For a review of current details on the extent of human rights abuses in ASEAN, see Human Rights Watch, *Human Rights in Southeast Asia: Briefing Materials for the ASEAN-Australia Summit*, Sydney, March 17–18, 2018.

2. Political, Economic, and Public Opinion Dimensions of Japan's China Policy

One of the key factors shaping the prospects of leveraging the U.S.-Japan alliance to compete with China in Southeast Asia is Japan's internal political environment, which affects both what the Self-Defense Forces (SDF) and Ministry of Defense are legally allowed to do under constitutional interpretations, as well as what they are able to do under policy guidance from the cabinet of Japan.[10] In this chapter, the author describes the key actors in Japan's political system and their attitudes toward important foreign and security policy issues, including the U.S.-Japan alliance and the issue of China. He then turns to the role of public opinion toward China as a separate consideration that will shape political leaders' calculations. Finally, he highlights the importance of China for key sectors of the Japanese economy, such as manufacturing, tourism, and education, that could serve to limit Japan's willingness to take costly steps to partner with the United States in competition with China in Southeast Asia.

Japan's Political Landscape Shapes the Country's Ability to Engage on National Security

Japan has a bicameral parliamentary system in which the major political party is the Liberal Democratic Party (LDP), a center-right party lead by Prime Minister Abe Shinzō that has controlled the government since December 2012 and for all but four years of the period from 1955 to 2019 (see Tables 2.1 and 2.2). The LDP is a large-tent political party that contains numerous factions, with some favoring a much more muscular foreign policy centered on revising the Constitution and building up the SDF's capabilities, others that are more focused on business interests and economic revitalization (including debt reduction), and yet others that are moved more by a desire to engage with China and manage bilateral and regional affairs from within the current framework of Japan's pacifist Constitution. The Abe administration generally tends to lean toward the first of those three approaches but has survived for so long by ensuring that all of the party's factions remain invested in the prime minister's continuance in power.

---

[10] Adam P. Liff, "Policy by Other Means: Collective Self-Defense and the Politics of Japan's Postwar Constitutional Reinterpretations," *Asia Policy*, No. 24, July 2017; Sheila A. Smith, *Japan Rearmed: The Politics of Military Power*, Cambridge, Mass.: Harvard University Press, 2019.

Table 2.1. Parties in the Lower House of the Diet

Party	Number of Members
Liberal Democratic Party	283
The Constitutional Democratic Party of Japan	68
Democratic Party for the People	40
Komeitō	29
Japanese Communist Party	12
Nippon Ishin (Japan Innovation Party)	11
The Reviewing Group on Social Security Policy	8
Social Democratic Party	2
The Party of Hope	2
Future Japan	2
Independents	8
Incumbents	465
Vacancies	0
Membership	465

SOURCE: House of Representatives, National Diet of Japan, "Strength of the In-House Groups of the House of Representatives," webpage, undated.

Table 2.2. Parties in the Upper House of the Diet

Party	Number of Members
Liberal Democratic Party and Voice of the People	123
The Constitutional Democratic Party of Japan and Minyukai and Hope Coalition	28
Democratic Party for the People and the Shin-Ryokufukai	27
Komeitō	25
Nippon Ishin (Japan Innovation Party) and the Party of Hope	15
Japanese Communist Party	14
Independents Club	2
Okinawa Whirlwind	2
Independents	3
Incumbents	239
Vacancies	3
Membership	242

SOURCE: House of Councillors, National Diet of Japan, "Strength of the Political Groups in the House of Councillors," webpage, undated.

As of this writing, the LDP rules in a coalition with the New Komei Party (Komeitō), a Buddhist-oriented party that is concerned primarily with education and pacifism and is less open to a more substantial role for Japan on the world stage, especially if that were to require a more active role for the SDF. The Komeitō is thus uncomfortable with the overall approach of the Abe administration to foreign and security policy and has portrayed itself as a brake on constitutional revision and faster steps to expand defense spending. As a result of its importance to the LDP in election mobilization, it has been able to slow and limit the shift toward a greater role for the SDF, while consenting to quietly support a more gradual defense buildup and expanded security cooperation with the United States and regional partners.

There are four main opposition parties to the governing LDP/Komeitō coalition, though their ability to compete effectively with the LDP has been limited since 2013, and their future prospects appear highly constrained as of late 2019.[11] The largest of these include the Constitutional Democratic Party (CDP) and the Democratic Party for the People (DPFP). From 2009 to 2012, the CDP and large segments of the DPFP were unified as the ruling (and now defunct) Democratic Party of Japan (DPJ). After the loss of power in December 2012, the party struggled to compete effectively, ultimately splintering over issues of electoral strategy and cooperation with other opposition parties, such as the Japan Communist Party (JCP) and the now defunct Party of Hope (Kibo no Tō), the latter of which merged with more-conservative members of the DPJ to form the DPFP. The CDP represents a stronger orientation toward public sector unions (and was the grouping within the DPJ that favored cooperation with the Communists in 2017), whereas the DPFP is more conservative and willing to countenance an expanded foreign and security profile for Japan.

The JCP represents the party most ideologically hostile to the Abe administration's goals of revising the Constitution and expanding Japan's ability to engage in defense cooperation with the United States or other actors; instead, the JCP favors emphasizing Japan's identity as a pacifist nation, scrapping the SDF entirely, and ending Japan's alliance with the United States.[12] The party's influence is seen most clearly in its interpolation of the administration in the Diet, as well as in its challenges to the relocation of Marine Corps Air Station Futenma in Okinawa to a new site in the prefecture around Henoko at Camp Schwab. It has also regularly complained about various U.S.-Japan training activities and filed several complaints about noise and pollution near U.S. military installations in Japan.[13]

The last of the four important opposition parties is the Japan Innovation Party, a regionally focused party based in Japan's second largest city of Osaka. The party originated in a call by local politicians for the central government in Tokyo to devolve political authority and decisionmaking down and out to the prefectures. Its leaders appeal to a mix of populism and

---

[11] Several other smaller parties also exist, but these are not strong enough to affect government policy on security issues in most cases.

[12] "Red Revival: Communists Become Japan's Strongest Political Opposition in the Provinces," *The Economist*, April 17, 2015.

[13] The author thanks Jim Schoff for recommending the inclusion of this point.

neoconservatism and favor a more muscular Japan, though they have also expelled a Diet member who openly wondered about the possibility of using force to recover Japan's territorial claims vis-à-vis Russia.[14]

As of early 2020, the LDP and its coalition partner, the New Kōmeitō, appeared to be well-positioned to continue to dominate Japanese politics over the near- to medium-term. As Figure 2.1 shows, by mid-2019, more than six and a half years into Abe's second stint in office, his cabinet support rate remained fairly stable, in the upper 40 percent to lower 50 percent range.[15]

Figure 2.1. Abe Shinzō Cabinet Approval Rate, 2013–2019

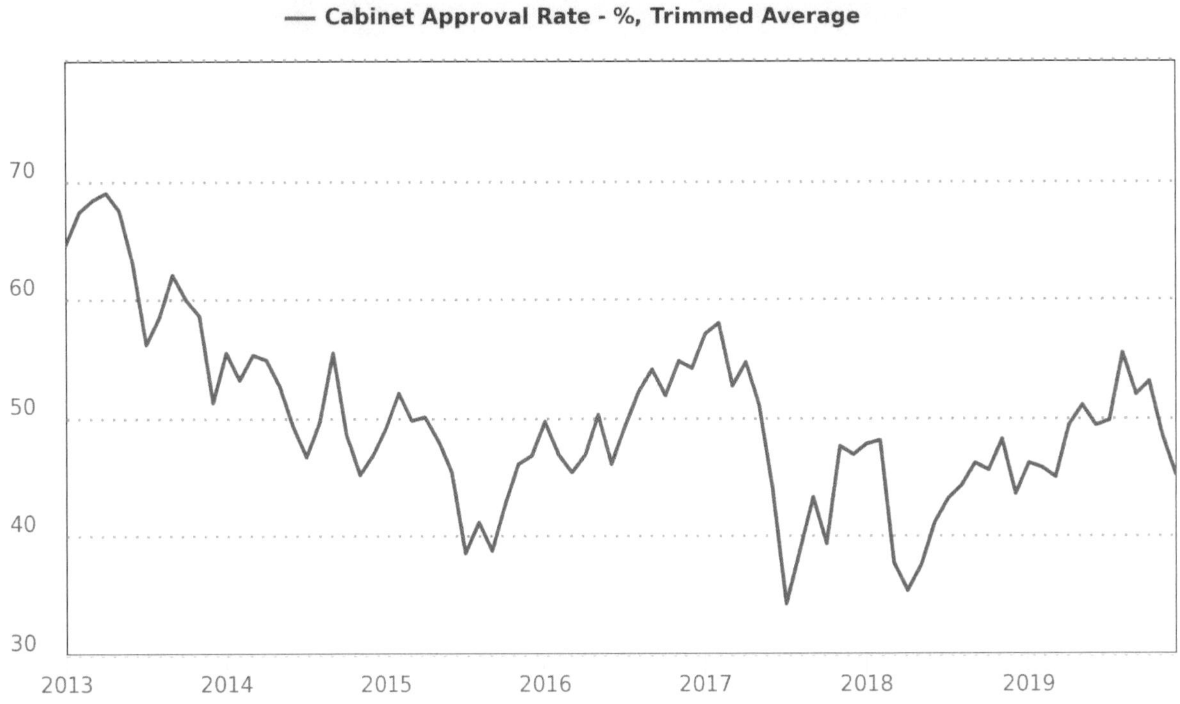

SOURCE: Japan Macro Advisors, 2019. Used with permission.

On November 20, 2019, Abe became the longest-serving prime minister in the history of Japan's constitutional government.[16] Survey data from the *Asahi Shimbun*, Japan's largest center-left newspaper, suggest that the leading opposition party, the Constitutional Democratic Party, enjoyed just a 5 percent support rate as of October 2018, down from its peak support rate

---

[14] Kyodo News, "Nippon Ishin no Kai Lawmaker Ousted from Party over Russia 'War' Gaffe," *Japan Times*, May 14, 2019.

[15] Japan Macro Advisors, "Cabinet Approval Rating," webpage, updated May 3, 2019.

[16] "Abe Shinzō Becomes Japan's Longest-Serving Prime Minister," Nippon Communications Foundation, November 20, 2019.

of just 17 percent.[17] Given that the opposition's public support rate remains weak and the next general election does not need to be called until October 22, 2021, Abe is well positioned to remain in office for some time to come, enabling his cabinet to continue to pursue the gradual strengthening of Japan's foreign and security cooperation with the United States. Most of the prospective successors to Abe—including (as of this writing) former Minister of Foreign Affairs and current LDP Policy Research Council chair Kishida Fumio, former Minister of Foreign Affairs and current Minister of Defense Kono Taro, former Minister of Defense Ishiba Shigeru, current Minister of the Environment Koizumi Shinjiro, and current Chief Cabinet Secretary Suga Yoshihide—share his pro-America views and his desire to strengthen Japan internally while expanding its regional and global roles externally, though no single leading candidate has yet emerged to serve as the leader-in-waiting.[18] Such an approach is also broadly supported by Japanese public opinion, which has been and remains consistently negative toward China and supportive of efforts to balance Beijing, as discussed in the next section.

Public Opinion Toward China Remains Extremely Negative

Since the mid-2000s, when China launched a major anti-Japan campaign domestically that was associated with an effort to mobilize opposition to Tokyo's efforts to promote United Nations (UN) Security Council (UNSC) reform with an eye toward gaining a permanent voice on the UNSC, Japanese public attitudes toward China have grown increasingly negative and have remained at a high level of disapproval. Beijing's coercive actions directed against Tokyo in 2010 and again in 2012 over China's claims to the Senkaku Islands only worsened and locked these attitudes in among Japanese survey respondents, whose opinions have shown little improvement since 2013 even as Chinese views of Japan have gradually improved (see Figure 2.2).[19]

Japan's negative views of China stem from several sources, some of which are related to China's direct disputes with (and treatment of) Japan and others that derive from the nature of the PRC's political system and its norm-violating behavior in the Indo-Pacific region (see Table 2.3).[20] By contrast, Japanese public opinion toward the United States has long been quite positive, with 67 percent of respondents expressing a "favorable" view in a 2018 Pew Research Center survey.[21]

---

[17] "Editorial: To Be a Viable Force, CDP Must Show Grassroots Identity," *Asahi Shimbun*, October 4, 2018.

[18] Author interviews with academics and government officials, Japan, April 2019.

[19] Genron NPO, *Japan-China Public Opinion Survey 2018*, Tokyo, October 2018.

[20] Genron NPO, 2018.

[21] Pew Research Center, "Global Indicators Database: Opinion of the United States: Japan," webpage, accessed January 20, 2020.

Figure 2.2. Japan-China Public Opinion Toward Other Country

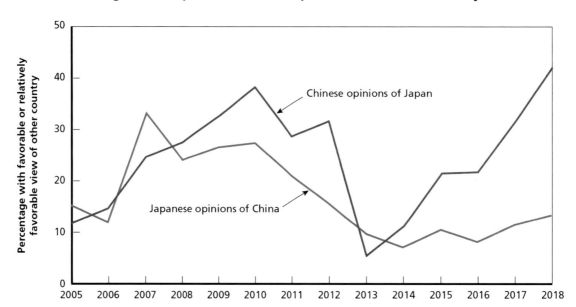

SOURCE: Adapted from Genron NPO, 2018, p. 5.

Table 2.3. Japanese Respondents' Reasons for Negative Views of China

Reason	2017 (*N* = 883)	2018 (*N* = 863)
Continuing territorial issues over Senkaku Islands and Japanese waters/airspace	56.7%	58.6%
Criticism of Japan over historical issues	46.4%	41.8%
Actions that go against international rules	40.2%	48.0%
Different political system (one-party rule of the Communist Party)	39.8%	37.0%
Aggressive acts by the Chinese as a world power in international society	34.4%	36.6%
Repeated anti-Japan broadcasts by the Chinese media	30.5%	28.6%
Notable military reinforcement and non-transparency	30.4%	33.5%
Incomprehensible patriotic actions and ideas	22.7%	22.4%
Entrenched nationalism of the Chinese people	16.1%	0.0%
Military conflict in the past	4.4%	4.3%
Other	6.2%	8.6%
No particular reason	6.0%	4.6%
No response	0.9%	0.7%

SOURCE: Genron NPO, 2018.

Some experts have argued that, despite these negative views of China, Japanese society at large has generally been reluctant to support a shift into outright competition with China, though others have identified Japanese foreign policy elites as more willing to engage in a "hard hedge" approach to managing China's growing challenges to regional order.[22] The Abe administration's policy statements have clearly indicated a willingness to push back against China more forcefully, and although the other major Japanese political parties have some differences on foreign policy, there is a fairly broad consensus (with the exception of the JCP) on the appropriateness of such a response.

One factor that the Abe cabinet or any other Japanese administration will bear in mind is the importance to Japan of its economic ties with China, which are explored in the next section.

China Is an Important Production Site and Market for Japan

Japan's trade and investment relationship with China and Hong Kong is substantial, with two-way trade in goods in 2018 topping just over US$350 billion, approximately US$178.5 billion of which was exports from Japan to China and Hong Kong and US$175.5 billion of which was imports from those two points of origin to Japan.[23]

Japanese firms have also been large investors in China, with cumulative foreign direct investment stock totaling just shy of US$500 billion by the close of 2018, with US$465.9 billion in China and another US$33 billion in Hong Kong.[24] Since the 1990s, many of Japan's largest firms have invested in production facilities in China, both to use the country as a lower-cost site for assembly for export and also to be closer to consumers in the China market, now the end destination for 73 percent of all output of Japanese-invested factories in China.[25] In the wake of growing tensions since 2005, Japanese firms have occasionally considered relocation to Southeast Asia, especially as Chinese labor costs have risen and as environmental pollution in China has worsened, but the China market remains important for Japan, and China also continues to be an important production site. Apart from brief spikes in the 2002–2005 and 2010–2013 time frames, Japanese foreign direct investment into China has generally held steady at around US$35–40 billion per year, a fact that has not changed despite the much larger size of the Chinese economy in 2018 as compared with 2002.[26]

One particularly important category of economic contacts between the two sides has been tourist arrivals from China to Japan, which topped 7.4 million in 2017, making China the number

---

[22] Sheila A. Smith, *Intimate Rivals: Japanese Domestic Politics and a Rising China*, New York: Columbia University Press, 2015; Jeffrey W. Hornung, "Japan's Growing Hard Hedge Against China," *Asian Security*, Vol. 10, No. 2, 2014.

[23] Japan External Trade Organization, "Japan's International Trade in Goods (Yearly): 2018", spreadsheet, 2019a.

[24] Japan External Trade Organization, "Japan's Outward and Inward Foreign Direct Investment: FDI Stock (Based on International Investment Position, Net), 1996–2018: Outward," spreadsheet, 2019b.

[25] Shintaro Terai and Yusuke Matsuzaki, "Japan's 'China-Heavy' Companies Take Larger Hit to Profits," *Nikkei Asian Review*, February 8, 2019.

[26] Kiyoyuki Seguchi, "FDI Toward China: Japanese Companies Becoming More Aggressive," Canon Institute for Global Studies, March 11, 2019.

one source of foreign visitors to the country.[27] Arrivals expanded further in 2018 to just shy of 8.4 million (see Figure 2.3).[28]

Figure 2.3. Tourist Arrivals to Japan by Country of Origin, 2018

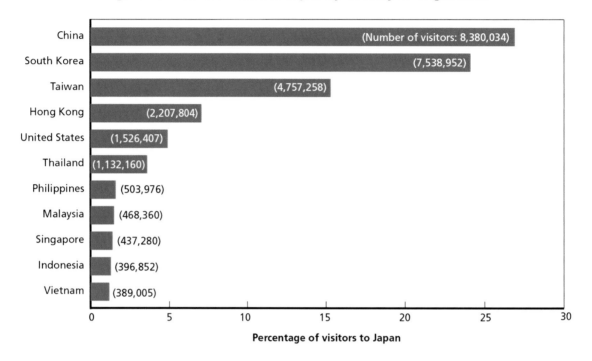

SOURCE: Japan National Tourism Organization (JNTO), "Japan Tourism Statistics: 2018 Breakdown by Country/Area," webpage, updated March 24, 2020.

Another important category of economic activity has been educational contacts. Japan's academic community generally views China as a valuable source of funding, given that the 107,260 Chinese students pursuing their education in Japan in 2017 constituted 40.2 percent of all international students enrolled in Japanese universities.[29]

Japanese media outlets have debated the importance of the growing numbers of Chinese tourists and students in recent years, with one report noting that in mid-2017 the number of short-term Chinese nationals in Japan had reached approximately 878,000, nearly tripling from just 320,000 in 2000 and in addition to the roughly 100,000 ethnically Chinese citizens of Japan.[30] Although PRC authors have tended to write about (and Chinese government policy has at times sought to leverage through normative appeals, bribery, or coercion) the global ethnic Chinese community as a vector for influence in foreign polities, Japan has not to date

---

[27] Daniel Hurst, "Amid Thaw, Japan Is Seeing a Boom in Chinese Tourists," *The Diplomat*, March 27, 2019.

[28] "Overseas Visitors to Japan in 2018 Top 31 Million," Nippon Communications Foundation, January 24, 2019.

[29] "Over 100,000 Chinese Studying in Japan," Nippon Communications Foundation, May 8, 2018.

[30] Mark Schreiber, "Media Stews over Growing Chinese Numbers in Japan," *Japan Times*, July 14, 2018.

experienced any noteworthy instances of suspected malign influence, political interference, or so-called *sharp power* from China directed at Tokyo via the ethnic Chinese community in Japan. A 2019 study tracked China's influence operations in Japan and noted that such operations might be directed at Okinawa as well as at any base activities across the Japanese archipelago more generally.[31]

Conclusion

Overall, the Japanese political landscape is dominated by a political party—the LDP—led by a powerful and durable political leader in Abe, who appears to face little substantial political opposition. Abe enjoys a generally strong political consensus on pushing back on China, undergirded by a largely supportive and China-skeptical public. The business, academic, and tourism communities will certainly continue to express an interest in stable and generally positive ties with China but are not likely to constrain the Abe administration in striving to balance China, provided this is done in ways that are not outright confrontational or ham-fisted. Although Chinese authors have sought to paint, and Chinese government policy has sought to exploit, global ethnic Chinese communities in the diaspora as vectors of influence for Beijing, to date these tactics do not appear to have been used inside Japan, nor (because of the relatively small number of ethnic Chinese citizens of Japan) would their sheer numbers appear to make this a promising avenue for Beijing to pursue.[32]

---

[31] Russell Hsiao, "A Preliminary Survey of CCP Influence Operations in Japan," *China Brief*, Vol. 19, No. 12, June 26, 2019.

[32] This comment is not intended to suggest that the ethnic Chinese community in Japan would be open to approaches China might try to employ to turn them into agents of influence. This report does not address the specific policy views of this narrow subset of the Japanese population, and therefore the author cannot characterize the views of its members. The author wishes to dispel, however, any possible inference or misimpression that mentioning this community reflects anything other than an acknowledgment that the PRC sees the global Chinese diaspora as one vector among many to extend its influence, without commenting on the reception such attempts might receive. For exemplary Chinese writings on exploiting the global Chinese diaspora as a vector of influence, see, among others, Xu Mei, "The Driving Force and Restraining Factors of Southeast Asian Chinese in the Promotion of Chinese Soft Power," *Southeast Asian Studies* (东南亚研究), Vol. 6, 2010; and Liu Juntao, "Overseas Chinese and Chinese Soft Power from the Economic Perspective: The Case of Indonesia," *Science-Economy-Society* (科学经济社会), No. 3, December 2012.

3. Japan's Evolving Security Policy and Response to Growing Chinese Capabilities and Assertiveness

In this chapter, the author briefly outlines the recent evolution of Japanese national security policy (paying particular attention to the factors driving Japan's defense modernization), the development of increasingly close military cooperation with the United States, and Japan's views of and expanding security ties with Southeast Asia.

Japan's Post–Cold War Defense Policy Evolving Toward Greater Flexibility, Capability

Since roughly 1990, Japan has watched with mounting concern as China's economic and military power has expanded, with implications for Beijing's aggressiveness in pursuing issues including the Senkaku Islands and broader control over the Ryukyu Islands; the two countries' dispute over undersea oil and gas resources in the East Sea; and the Chinese People's Liberation Army's (PLA's) ability to threaten Japanese sea lines of communication, air sovereignty, and maritime security, as well as its growing ability to target U.S. bases in Japan and its use of cyber operations against Japan.[33]

In 1997, in response to the 1994 first North Korean nuclear crisis and the 1995–1996 Taiwan Strait Crisis, the United States and Japan updated their defense guidelines to explicitly capture Japan's role in "situations in areas surrounding Japan."[34] Subsequently, in light of the growth of North Korean and Chinese ballistic missile capabilities, especially in the wake of North Korea's 1998 launch of a Taepodong that overflew Japan, the United States and Japan initiated joint research and development of ballistic missile defense capabilities.[35]

Although Japan hoped to engage with China throughout the late 1990s and early 2000s and, in so doing, reduce the prospects of conflict and confrontation, Beijing reacted negatively to visits by then Prime Minister Koizumi Junichiro to the controversial Yasukuni Shrine in the early 2000s and Japan's 2005 quest for a permanent seat on the UNSC by initiating a domestic anti-Japan campaign that spurred nationalist sentiment and served to sour relations.[36] During his first

---

[33] Chinese military capabilities are detailed in Ministry of Defense of Japan, *Defense of Japan 2019*, Tokyo, 2019, pp. 57–91.

[34] Ministry of Foreign Affairs of Japan, *The Guidelines for Japan-U.S. Defense Cooperation*, April 27, 2015.

[35] Michael D. Swaine, Rachel M. Swanger, and Takashi Kawakami, *Japan and Ballistic Missile Defense*, Santa Monica, Calif.: RAND Corporation, MR-1374-CAPP, 2001.

[36] Richard C. Bush, *The Perils of Proximity: China-Japan Security Relations*, Washington, D.C.: Brookings Institution Press, 2010; Smith, 2015.

term as prime minister in 2006, Abe sought to repair ties by making China his first overseas trip after assuming the post. Furthermore, a June 2008 agreement to try to resolve the two sides' dispute over subsurface oil and gas resources in the East China Sea ultimately foundered on Chinese noncompliance and lack of commitment, something many Japanese worry carries implications for Japan's broader maritime and energy security.[37]

From 2010 to 2012, Japan's view of China shifted dramatically following a pair of incidents around the Senkaku Islands (which China belatedly laid claim to in the wake of a 1969 UN panel report speculating that they might contain undersea resources). In 2010, a drunk Chinese fishing boat captain twice rammed Japan Coast Guard vessels engaged in maritime law enforcement operations around the Senkakus, leading to a several-week-long diplomatic standoff, during which China cut off rare earth exports to Japan. In 2012, when the Japanese central government decided to purchase the three privately owned islands in the Senkaku chain so as to prevent the governor of Tokyo Municipality, Ishihara Shintaro, from buying them and undertaking provocative actions (such as engaging in construction or permitting tourism), China responded with a dramatic uptick in the number of fishing and China Coast Guard intrusions into the waters around the islands, including the 12-nautical-mile territorial sea. Additionally, Beijing permitted and encouraged several riots targeting Japanese institutions (companies, diplomatic facilities, etc.), resulting in damages of more than US$100 million, as well as several injuries.[38] Since that time, despite Japanese efforts to manage the relationship with China to achieve more-cooperative outcomes, China has largely resisted improving ties, a development that has frustrated many in Tokyo but has also revealed how resistant Japan is to transform its ties with China into an outright competition or confrontation.[39]

In response, successive Japanese administrations have increased defense budgets, reoriented defense strategy, procured new military capabilities, and adopted a more activist foreign policy oriented toward constraining China's ability to reshape the region in ways that threaten Japan's interests, what one expert has called a "hard hedge."[40] In 2010, the Kan Naoto administration of the DPJ released a new set of National Defense Program Guidelines (NDPG), which replaced Japan's previous "Basic Defense Force Concept" (an approach focused on the static defense of Japan against a Soviet ground invasion from the north) with a "Dynamic Defense" approach that sought to respond to Chinese air and maritime threats and North Korean ballistic missile

---

[37] James Manicom, *Bridging Troubled Waters: China, Japan, and Maritime Order in the East China Sea*, Washington, D.C.: Georgetown University Press, 2014.

[38] Agence France-Presse, "China Anti-Japan Protest Damage May Be Over US$100M," *South China Morning Post*, November 13, 2012.

[39] Smith, 2015.

[40] Hornung, 2014.

challenges originating from Japan's south and west.[41] When the DPJ fell from power in late 2012 to the LDP, the Abe administration issued a new NDPG in late 2013 that carried forward much of the previous defense guidance but added the importance of creating a "dynamic joint defense" focusing on generating deterrence through coordinated efforts across Ground, Air, and Maritime Self-Defense Forces and in tandem with the armed forces of the United States.[42] Additionally, Japan's security strategy focus under the Abe administration is premised on a three-part approach that involves (1) self-strengthening, (2) deepening alliance cooperation with the United States, and (3) expanding cooperation with regional partners and institutions in the Asia-Pacific.[43] As the 2013 NDPG explains, in pursuit of the third leg of this approach, "together with the Japan-U.S. alliance, a security network needs to be created . . . [and] Japan will . . . maintain and enhance security cooperation with the Association of Southeast Asian Nations (ASEAN) countries."[44]

Following China's December 2013 unilateral announcement of an Air Defense Identification Zone (ADIZ) that covered the Senkaku Islands, Japan sought and received a verbal commitment from President Barack Obama in April 2014 that Article 5 of the U.S.-Japan Security Treaty covered Japan's administrative control over those islands. Shortly thereafter, Japan reinterpreted the implications of Article 9 of its Constitution so as to permit the exercise of the inherent right of collective self-defense (CSD). In April 2015, the United States and Japan completed work on and released a new set of *Guidelines for Japan-U.S. Defense Cooperation* that focused on expanding the alliance's focus to include "cooperation with regional and other partners, as well as international organizations" to reflect the "global nature of the Japan-U.S. alliance," one aim of which would be to "cooperate to the maximum extent practicable" on international activities. The types of activities listed by the *Guidelines* include UN peacekeeping operations, international HA/DR operations, maritime security, partner capacity-building, noncombatant evacuation, ISR operations, training and exercises, logistics support, and trilateral and multilateral cooperation, among other aspects outlined.[45] In September 2015, the Abe administration put forward and passed a raft of measures dubbed the Legislation for Peace and Security that operationalized a wider array of activities by the SDF, including counterpiracy operations, de-mining activities, ballistic missile defense, noncombatant evacuation operations for Japanese citizens in harm's way overseas, and data collection about foreign air forces' operations relevant to the security of Japan, many of which could be relevant should the United

---

[41] Government of Japan, *National Defense Program Guidelines for FY 2011 and Beyond*, Tokyo, December 17, 2010.

[42] Government of Japan, *National Defense Program Guidelines for FY 2014 and Beyond*, Tokyo, December 17, 2013, p. 7.

[43] Onodera Itsunori, "Strengthening Japan's Defense Force," *Asia-Pacific Review*, Vol. 20, No. 2, 2013.

[44] Government of Japan, 2013, pp. 8–9.

[45] Ministry of Foreign Affairs of Japan, 2015.

States or the United States and Japan become involved in a conflict with China in Southeast Asia or in the South China Sea.[46] Still, it is important to recognize that Japan is still highly constrained in its ability to engage in CSD and that, in order to do so, the prime minister must find that Japan's survival must be at risk, no other means is available to address this risk, and the force used by Japan must be the minimum necessary.[47]

For these reasons, much of Japan's efforts to balance China have focused on articulating diplomatic and normative frameworks that can be paired with economic and security (as opposed to defense) cooperation. For example, in August 2016, at the Sixth Tokyo International Conference on African Development, Prime Minister Abe articulated his administration's "free and open Indo-Pacific" (FOIP) vision premised on a "policy of Proactive Contribution to Peace" through international cooperation.[48] The Abe administration moved quickly to operationalize the international security cooperation aspects of FOIP in November 2016 by announcing its "Vientiane Vision" for defense cooperation with ASEAN during then Minister of Defense Inada Tomomi's visit to the Lao People's Democratic Republic. Tokyo's approach involves several lines of effort. First, Japan vowed to support a regional order based on the principles of international law and offered support to ASEAN in that organization's efforts to maintain such an order, especially in the realms of air and maritime law. Second, in addition to articulating an attractive normative stance intended to woo Southeast Asian states, Tokyo offered to assist ASEAN efforts to build up its member states' ISR and air and maritime search and rescue capabilities. Third, Japan extended offers of practical training on landmine clearing and unexploded ordnance disposal, HA/DR operations, participation in UN peacekeeping, cybersecurity, and defense planning, as well as human resource development and defense industrial cooperation. Finally, Japan extended an invitation to ASEAN members to deepen training and exercises and increase exchanges of opinion leaders and defense policymakers.[49]

Continuing its push to sustain and build a viable regional order premised on resisting coercion and requiring countries to abide by international law in peacefully resolving their disputes, Japanese officials in November 2017 met with their American, Australian, and Indian counterparts on the sidelines of the 31st ASEAN Summit in Manila, where the four countries vowed to reestablish the Quadrilateral Dialogue Mechanism.[50] In December 2018, Japan further refined its defense strategy, releasing a new NDPG as well as the five-year *Medium Term*

---

[46] Ministry of Defense of Japan, *Defense of Japan White Paper 2016*, Tokyo, 2016a.

[47] Michael Green and Jeffrey W. Hornung, "Ten Myths About Japan's Collective Self-Defense Change," *The Diplomat*, July 10, 2014.

[48] Ministry of Foreign Affairs of Japan, *Diplomatic Bluebook 2017*, Tokyo, 2017a, p. 192.

[49] Ministry of Defense of Japan, "Vientiane Vision: Japan's Defense Cooperation Initiative with ASEAN," Tokyo, 2016b.

[50] Ministry of Foreign Affairs of Japan, *Australia-India-Japan-U.S. Consultations on the Indo-Pacific*, press release, Tokyo, November 12, 2017d.

Defense Program, which outlined spending and procurement plans in support of the new defense strategy. Noting that the "security environment surrounding Japan is changing at extremely high speeds," the NDPG nonetheless reiterated Tokyo's commitment to self-strengthening, tightening alliance bonds with the United States, and deepening cooperation with international partners.[51] With respect to ASEAN specifically, the NDPG noted that

> Japan will continue to support efforts for strengthening the centrality and unity of the Association of Southeast Asian Nations (ASEAN), which is the key to regional cooperation, and promote practical bilateral and multilateral cooperation, including joint training and exercises, defense equipment and technology cooperation, and capacity building assistance.[52]

The *Medium Term Defense Program* further commented on this, noting that Japan would prioritize joint training and exercises, equipment and technology cooperation, capacity-building assistance, maritime security, international peace cooperation activities, and arms control, disarmament, and nonproliferation.[53]

China Is a Key Factor Driving the Evolution of Japanese Defense Policy

Major issues for Japanese national security and defense policy today involve three main concerns. First, as outlined above, the threat posed by China is the primary concern driving much of Japan's defense modernization and the evolution of Tokyo's national security strategy and policymaking. The China threat can be further broken down into a conventional military challenge and the challenge posed by China's use of *gray zone coercion*, or the employment of measures that fall short of force but are designed to change the status quo without triggering a conflict, across a variety of dimensions.

For the conventional threat, Tokyo continues to modernize its ground, air, surface, subsurface, ballistic missile defense, and command, control, communications, computers, intelligence, surveillance, and reconnaissance (C4ISR) systems to meet the growing military capabilities of the PLA. Recent upgrades to the SDF have included the build-out of a network of ground-based sensors, surface-to-air missiles, and antiship cruise missiles across the Southwest Islands (Ryukyus) intended to turn China's anti-access/area denial (A2/AD) strategy back on the PLA should it seek to coerce Japan.[54] Additionally, Tokyo has

- upgraded the Japan Air Self-Defense Force's (JASDF's) air fleet by purchasing 105 F-35As and 42 F-35Bs

---

[51] Government of Japan, *National Defense Program Guidelines for FY 2019 and Beyond*, Tokyo, December 18, 2018b, p. 1.

[52] Government of Japan, 2018b, p. 16.

[53] Government of Japan, *Medium Term Defense Program (FY2019–FY2023)*, Tokyo, December 18, 2018a.

[54] Toshi Yoshihara, *Going Anti-Access at Sea: How Japan Can Turn the Tables on China*, Washington, D.C.: Center for a New American Security, September 2014.

- announced plans to repurpose the *Izumo*-class helicopter destroyer for fixed-wing air operations of the F-35B
- expanded the Japan Maritime Self-Defense Force's (JMSDF's) submarine fleet by six boats
- indicated its intent to acquire three Global Hawk high-altitude and long endurance airborne ISR airframes
- announced plans to procure two Aegis Ashore missile defense batteries and field them by 2023.

In terms of the PRC's gray zone coercion, Tokyo has been dealing with increased airborne intrusions into Japan's ADIZ (see Figure 3.1), increased intrusions into the waters around the Senkakus (see Figure 3.2), and continuing high levels of cyber intrusions suspected to be linked to China. Japan's main responses to these intrusions have been (1) to build up its forces, (2) to attempt to surmount the institutional divide between the SDF and the Japan Coast Guard (which falls not under the Ministry of Defense but under the civilian Ministry of Land, Infrastructure, and Transportation), and (3) to further deepen security cooperation with the United States. The last of these responses has been pursued primarily by eliciting continuing statements of support from Washington, including then Secretary of Defense James Mattis in 2017, and by following through on the revised Guidelines for Japan-U.S. Defense Cooperation of 2015, which established an Alliance Coordination Mechanism to ensure a "seamless" response to gray zone coercion.[55]

Figure 3.1. Japanese Scrambles Against Chinese Aircraft

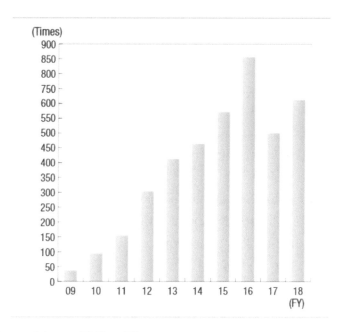

SOURCE: Ministry of Defense of Japan, 2019, p. 75.

---

[55] DoD, "Joint Press Briefing by Secretary Mattis and Minister Inada, Tokyo Japan," transcript, February 4, 2017.

Figure 3.2. Chinese Vessels in Waters Surrounding the Senkaku Islands

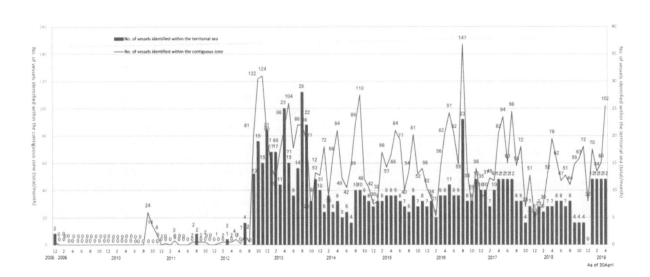

SOURCE: Ministry of Foreign Affairs of Japan, "Trends in Chinese Government and Other Vessels in the Waters Surrounding the Senkaku Islands, and Japan's Response," webpage, undated.

A second source of security threats to Japan stems from the Democratic People's Republic of Korea. Tokyo worries about the North Korean regime's growing ballistic and cruise missile portfolio, its expanding nuclear arsenal, Pyongyang's willingness to send special operations forces and state agents abroad to employ other weapons of mass destruction (as evidenced by the assassination of Kim Jong Un's half-brother Kim Jong Nam in Kuala Lumpur International Airport in early 2017), and North Korea's growing use of cyber operations for intelligence-gathering, illicit revenue generation (through bank heists and ransomware), and coercion (most notably, the Sony Pictures attack).[56]

A final source of concern for Japan has been the possibility of allied abandonment by the United States. This issue dates back to the early 1970s, with President Richard Nixon's "shock" announcement of the normalization of relations with China (for which Tokyo was not given advance warning). It took on renewed importance during the trade tensions of the 1980s and was revived in the late 1990s when President Bill Clinton's trip to China did not include a stopover in Japan either on the way out or on the way back (leading to the rise of concerns about "Japan passing"). The 2008 removal of North Korea from the state sponsors of terrorism list despite Pyongyang's failure to account for kidnapped Japanese citizens (something the Bush administration was perceived to have promised Tokyo) also aggravated such concerns, as did the

---

[56] Jenny Jun, Scott LaFoy, and Ethan Sohn, *North Korea's Cyber Operations: Strategy and Responses*, Washington, D.C.: Center for Strategic and International Studies, December 2015; Emma Chanlett-Avery, Liana W. Rosen, John W. Rollins, and Catherine A. Theohary, *North Korean Cyber Capabilities: In Brief*, Washington, D.C.: Congressional Research Service, R44912, August 3, 2017; Matthew Ha and David Maxwell, *Kim Jong Un's "All-Purpose Sword": North Korean Cyber-Enabled Economic Warfare*, Washington, D.C.: Foundation for Defense of Democracies, October 2018.

Obama administration's short-lived second-term flirtation with the Chinese concept of a "new type of great power relations" and its consideration of the possibility of moving to a declared "no first use" policy for nuclear weapons.[57]

Since 2010, these concerns have fueled Japan's efforts to bind itself ever more closely to the United States through significant arms purchases, reforms to the guidelines for U.S.-Japan defense cooperation, a growing military budget, enhanced political-diplomatic cooperation and coordination, and efforts to ensure that the region's international organizational architecture includes a place for Washington. Such concerns grew as a consequence of (1) comments during the 2016 presidential campaign by then candidate Donald J. Trump, (2) the Trump administration's decision to withdraw from the Trans-Pacific Partnership, (3) its imposition of steel tariffs on U.S. allies (including Japan), and (4) several remarks by Trump that seem to continue to question the value to the United States of alliances in general and the U.S.-Japan alliance in particular.[58] For these reasons, the Abe administration has sought to build a close personal relationship between the prime minister and the president, with Abe visiting New York during the period between Trump's election in 2016 and his inauguration in 2017 and meeting with or talking to the president numerous times since then.

Regarding China and the United States, Japan seeks to strike a delicate balance, one paradoxically made both easier and more challenging in light of current circumstances. For example, Tokyo has been heartened to see the United States under the Trump administration recognize a greater degree of competitive threat from China and appreciates that this recognition means that Washington is less likely to prioritize cooperation with Beijing over Tokyo.[59] On the other hand, Japanese policymakers and analysts continue to harbor concerns that the Trump administration might adopt a "transactional" approach to foreign policy that would enable Beijing to outmaneuver Tokyo by offering up some unexpected but politically desirable outcome that Washington would value. Additionally, although Japanese elites hope the United States will stand up to China, there are some who hope the United States can do so without forcing countries in the region to openly choose between the United States and China, while others worry that Washington could provoke a state of outright competition, confrontation, conflict, or war with Beijing.[60]

As the United States began to adopt the Abe administration's language about FOIP, Tokyo began to shift slightly in its emphasis.[61] As of this writing, the Abe administration continues to talk about FOIP but increasingly describes it as a vision instead of a strategy over fears that the

---

[57] Smith, 2019.

[58] Jennifer Jacobs, "Trump Muses Privately About Ending Postwar Japan Defense Pact," Bloomberg, June 24, 2019.

[59] Author interviews with Japanese academics, think-tank experts, and government officials, Tokyo, April 2019.

[60] Smith, 2019; author interviews with Japanese academics, think-tank experts, and government officials, Tokyo, April 2019.

[61] Author interview with Japanese government official in Tokyo, April 2019.

language of strategy might not be acceptable to the Southeast Asian nations that the concept is intended to appeal to, many leaders of which appear to think a strategy implies an intent to confront or contain China. Additionally, recognizing that many Southeast Asian nations are only marginally democratic at best and that other Southeast Asian nations that Tokyo and Washington might want to appeal to would regard democracy as downright threatening, Japanese policymakers have increasingly talked about their vision as being one of a "free, open, and *inclusive* Indo-Pacific."[62] The addition of *inclusive* is intended both to dilute any concerns that Tokyo might be pushing countries to democratize and to signal that Japan's approach is welcoming of China, *if* Beijing plays by the same rules that others are expected to abide by.[63]

Japan Has Few Formal Defense Relations with China

Although Japan has had formal diplomatic relations with China since 1972, the two sides have very few contacts in the way of military-to-military ties. Japan neither buys nor sells arms to China, nor does it engage in defense industrial co-development. It does not share intelligence with China, nor does it provide logistics support to the PLA.[64] To date, no joint exercises have been held, though the two sides have occasional contact at multilateral military exercises, such as the 2014 and 2016 Rim of the Pacific exercises, and Japan sent a warship to participate in the PLA Navy's 70th anniversary event in 2019, though this was the first JMSDF vessel to visit China since 2011.[65]

Since its founding, the PRC has sought to constrain Japan's rearmament and subsequent military development, regularly complaining about Japanese "remilitarization" and warning about the impending "return of Japanese militarism." In 2015, Chinese propaganda sought to play up the notion that Japan was trying to overturn the antifascist victory in World War II by loosening constraints on the SDF's ability to engage in collective self-defense and developing ambitions to become a military power once more.[66]

At the level of defense ministers, the two sides have very infrequent contact, with an extended gap in direct communications of four years and five months from August 2011 to November 2015, and another gap of three years from 2015 to 2018.[67] In addition to senior contacts, Japan's Sasakawa Peace Foundation, a private nongovernmental organization, has

---

[62] Author interview with Japanese government official in Tokyo, April 2019.

[63] Brad Glosserman, "FOIP Has a Problem with 'Free,'" Pacific Forum, PacNet No. 9, January 29, 2019; author interviews with Japanese foreign policy experts, Tokyo, April 2019.

[64] Ministry of Defense of Japan, 2019.

[65] Ben Blanchard, "Indian, Australian Warships Arrive in China for Naval Parade," Reuters, April 20, 2019.

[66] Wang Meiping, "Abe Speech to Indicate Japan's Future," *China Daily*, April 21, 2015.

[67] Ministry of Defense of Japan, *Defense of Japan 2018*, Tokyo, 2018; Isabel Reynolds, "Japan, China Defense Ministers Meet for First Time in 3 Years," Bloomberg, October 19, 2018.

facilitated field grade officer exchanges between the SDF and the PLA, most recently in February 2018.[68]

In addition, military-to-military contacts between the two sides have been constrained by the fact that the Chinese refused for over a decade (from 2007 to 2018) to conclude an agreement establishing a military crisis management mechanism that could link the two sides, holding out in an apparent effort to try to extract something from Japan.[69] As the PLA increasingly operates in proximity to Japan—transiting through various straits of the Japanese archipelago and flying into Japan's ADIZ (see Figure 3.3), as well as intruding into the Senkakus with its government-linked nonmilitary vessels and fishing fleet—Japan has placed an increasing emphasis on the importance of such a hotline, which China agreed to in principle in 2008 but refused to actually implement for a decade.[70]

According to the *Defense of Japan 2018* white paper, the main components of the Maritime and Aerial Communication Mechanism that Tokyo and Beijing signed in May 2018 include "(1) annual and expert meetings between the two countries' defense authorities, (2) a hotline between Japanese and Chinese defense authorities, and (3) on scene communication measures between vessels and aircrafts of the SDF and the People's Liberation Army."[71]

As the foregoing review of Japanese perceptions of China's military challenge shows, the rise of a more capable and more aggressive PLA has been a major driver of Japanese military modernization and strategy development, while military-to-military contacts with the PRC have played little to no role in restraining Japanese counterbalancing behavior, since China has left these contacts underdeveloped. To be sure, Japan has sought to focus most of its hedging or balancing efforts close to home, focusing on the four main islands (Hokkaido, Honshu, Shikoku, and Kyushu) and the development of a "Southwestern Wall strategy" in the Ryukyu Island chain supported by the development of new capabilities, facilities, and posture arrangements designed to enhance deterrence and defenses along the Ryukyus and around the Senkakus.[72] More recently, however, Japan has begun to countenance an expanded effort to engage Southeast Asia using the SDF, in addition to more-traditional efforts to transfer nonlethal capabilities and training. Although Japan is certain to continue to place the highest priority on homeland defense, the prospects for an expanded role for Japanese defense cooperation with the United States in Southeast Asia are nonetheless quite good, as discussed in the next chapter.

---

[68] Ministry of Defense of Japan, 2018.

[69] Shannon Tiezzi, "China, Japan Close to Crisis Management Breakthrough," *The Diplomat*, March 4, 2015.

[70] "Japan and China Agree on Security Hotline After a Decade of Talks," Reuters, May 9, 2018.

[71] Ministry of Defense of Japan, 2018, p. 362.

[72] Koichiro Bansho "Japan's New Defense Strategy in the Southwest Islands and Development of Amphibious Operations Capabilities," in Scott W. Harold, Koichiro Bansho, Jeffrey W. Hornung, Koichi Isobe, and Richard L. Simcock II, *The U.S.-Japan Alliance Conference: Meeting the Challenge of Amphibious Operations*, Santa Monica, Calif.: RAND Corporation, CF-387-GOJ, 2018.

Figure 3.3. Chinese Military Operations in Air and Maritime Spaces Near Japan

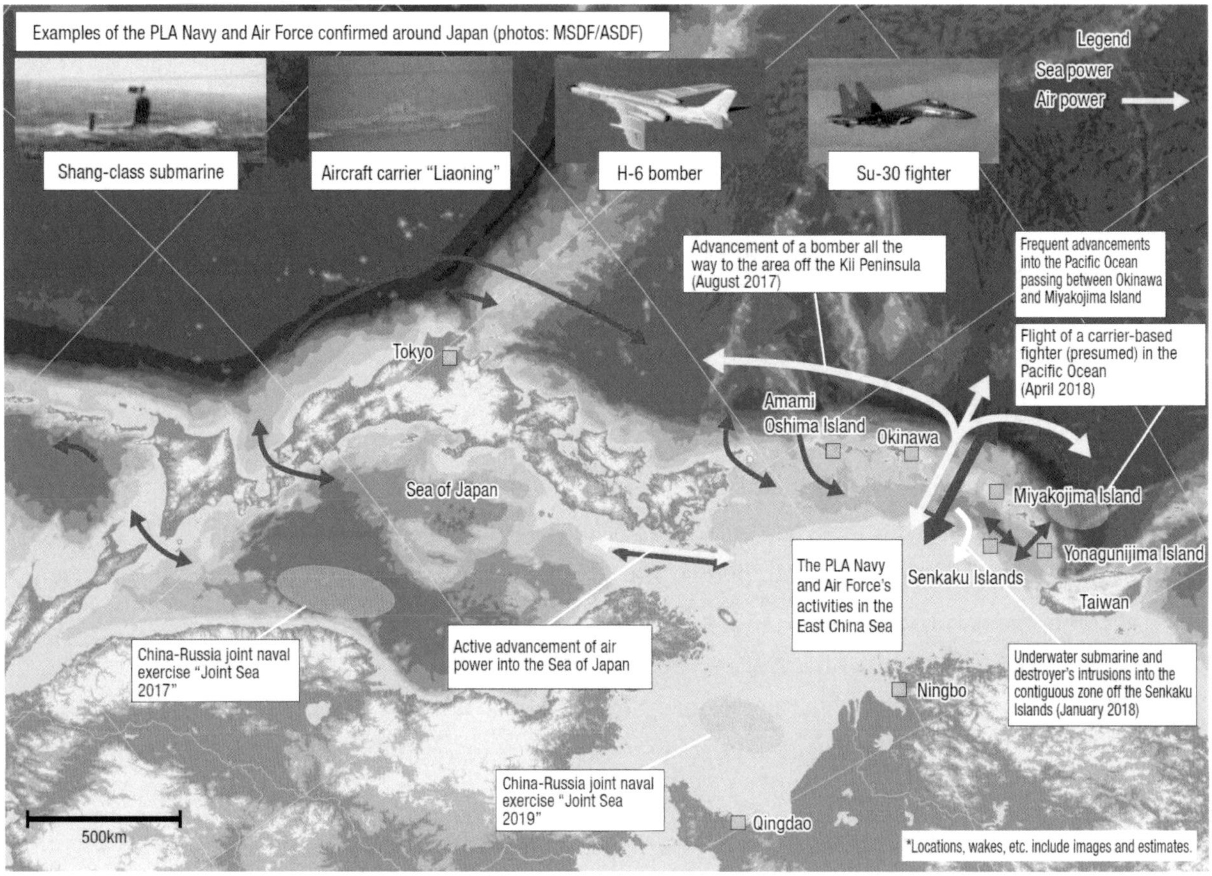

Examples of the PLA Navy and Air Force confirmed around Japan (photos: MSDF/ASDF)

Shang-class submarine
Aircraft carrier "Liaoning"
H-6 bomber
Su-30 fighter

Legend
Sea power
Air power

Advancement of a bomber all the way to the area off the Kii Peninsula (August 2017)

Frequent advancements into the Pacific Ocean passing between Okinawa and Miyakojima Island

Flight of a carrier-based fighter (presumed) in the Pacific Ocean (April 2018)

Tokyo

Amami Oshima Island
Okinawa

Sea of Japan

Miyakojima Island

Yonagunijima Island

The PLA Navy and Air Force's activities in the East China Sea

Senkaku Islands

Taiwan

China-Russia joint naval exercise "Joint Sea 2017"

Active advancement of air power into the Sea of Japan

Ningbo

Underwater submarine and destroyer's intrusions into the contiguous zone off the Senkaku Islands (January 2018)

China-Russia joint naval exercise "Joint Sea 2019"

500km

Qingdao

*Locations, wakes, etc. include images and estimates.

SOURCE: Ministry of Defense of Japan, 2019, p. 75.

Conclusion

As the China threat to Japan's security has evolved, Japan has responded by self-strengthening, tightening alliance relations with the United States, and expanding its contributions to regional order, institutions, and efforts to bolster status quo–oriented partners. As will be discussed in the next chapter, it is this last effort—Japan's expanding security cooperation with Asian partners, especially in Southeast Asia—that makes it an especially attractive partner for the United States, DoD, and the USAF.

4. Japanese Defense Relations with Southeast Asia

In this chapter, the author looks at Japan's defense cooperation with Southeast Asia and how Japan and the United States might deepen military cooperation in Southeast Asia.

Some scholars have cautioned that, even in the wake of Japan's 2014 decision to reinterpret Article 9 of the Constitution as permitting the exercise of the inherent right of collective self-defense, the 2015 revision of the *Guidelines for Japan-U.S. Defense Cooperation*, and the passage of the 2015 Peace and Security legislation, Japan is still extraordinarily constrained in what it can do together with the United States in the defense realm.[73] Even with the loosening of policy constraints on Japan's exercise of the inherent right of collective self-defense, one interviewee contended, "Our hands are still relatively tied . . . our goals in Southeast Asia should be to increase transparency [and situational awareness among partners] and to maintain a steady presence and pace of activities."[74] Another interviewee aptly pointed out that "the Japan Self-Defense Forces, the general public, and politicians are all getting used to regional deployments [and expanded defense cooperation] just like they got used to collective self-defense and Japan's participation in United Nations peacekeeping operations . . . people thought that these were impossible, but they were not [and neither is a greater role for Japan in regional defense cooperation]."[75]

As this last comment suggests, there are indeed some areas in which cooperation can be deepened, and although many of these build on preexisting Japanese defense and security engagement with the region, some might go beyond what is currently seen as politically feasible if the groundwork is laid in a step-by-step process in tandem with the United States. "We need to focus on efficient capacity-building, and efficient capacity-building means capacity-building that is coordinated with the United States," one interviewee argued.[76] "To block China's expansion in Southeast Asia," another expert remarked,

> we need to shape regional countries' perceptions, confidence, and sense of being supported . . . we should provide tacit support implying a willingness to come in [with expanded aid and assistance] if matters escalate . . . [The region's support is critical because] if the Philippines and Vietnam stop contesting China's escalating militarization of the South China Sea, then any ideas the U.S. has about 'distributed basing' won't work.[77]

---

[73] Jeffrey W. Hornung and Mike M. Mochizuki, "Japan: Still an Exceptional U.S. Ally," *Washington Quarterly*, Vol. 39, No. 1, 2016.

[74] Author interview with Japanese government official, Tokyo, April 2019.

[75] Author interview with Japanese think-tank official, Tokyo, April 2019.

[76] Author interview with Japanese government official, Tokyo, April 2019.

[77] Author interview with Japanese government official, Tokyo, April 2019.

These opportunities for expanded defense cooperation are explored below following an initial discussion of how the two sides see the region and a description of Japan's defense and security cooperation with Southeast Asia to date.

U.S. and Japanese Priority Relationships with Southeast Asia Overlap Substantially

U.S. defense policy relationships in Southeast Asia center on U.S. alliances with the Philippines and Thailand, together with a close partnership with Singapore and growing strategic relationships with Indonesia and Vietnam. U.S. defense policy toward the region aims to promote "preparedness," "partnerships," and a "networked region" in support of the goals of "deterring aggression, maintaining stability, and ensuring free access to the global commons."[78]

According to extensive interviews with Japanese officials and foreign and defense policy experts, three to six Southeast Asian countries are strategic priorities. In rough, unofficial order of priority, these are the Philippines, Vietnam, and Indonesia, then Malaysia, Singapore, and Thailand; Burma, Brunei, Cambodia, and Laos round out the rest of Southeast Asia but are low priorities (see Figure 4.1). In addition to the description of Japan's view of security ties with Southeast Asian nations described in the *Defense of Japan* white papers over the years, the priority ranking in Figure 4.1 also reflects Japan's actual engagement with these nations to date.

Figure 4.1. Priority Security Cooperation Countries for Japan

Japan

Top	Indonesia, Philippines, Vietnam
Middle	Malaysia, Singapore, Thailand
Low	Burma, Brunei, Cambodia, Laos

SOURCES: Ministry of Defense of Japan, 2018; author interviews with Japanese government officials and military officers, Tokyo, April 2019.

Several Japanese interlocutors expressed the view that the Philippines is the most important of these countries to Japan because of its status as a U.S. ally and its proximity to Taiwan, though one interviewee argued that Thailand is the key because it has the biggest economy in mainland Southeast Asia, has the most military capabilities, and is being the most actively targeted by China in an attempt to pull it away from the U.S.-linked order.[79] Officially, the

---

[78] DoD, 2019.

[79] Author interview with Japanese government official, Tokyo, April 2019.

Defense of Japan 2018 discussion of cooperation and exchanges with Southeast Asia begins with Indonesia, moves on to Vietnam, and then discusses Singapore and the Philippines before turning to Thailand, Cambodia, Myanmar, Laos, Malaysia, and Brunei.[80]

Japan has long sought to establish political-diplomatic and soft-power influence in Southeast Asia, the region Tokyo regards as the most strategically relevant to competing with China to enhance its security.[81] The goal of Japanese policy is to prevent China from achieving regional hegemony over Southeast Asia and to forestall China from establishing dominance over the South China Sea. As one interviewee stated, in Japanese thinking, Southeast Asia is the "soft flank confronting China's air and maritime power," which is why Japan has focused its defense cooperation efforts, in part, on building up air and maritime domain awareness and training regional militaries on their rights and China's obligations under international law.[82]

Key Japanese interlocutors warn that "China's influence in Southeast Asia is overtaking the combined influence of the U.S. and Japan" and that, to respond effectively, Washington and Tokyo must approach the region in an increasingly coordinated and planned way, with "the division of labor on engagement with the region" as the key.[83] Another interviewee echoed this view, arguing that "in mainland Southeast Asia we're already behind; in maritime Southeast Asia we're currently either stronger or at par with China but in the long run we will be overrun" if present trends continue on their existing trajectories.[84]

However, Japanese experts and government officials caution that the United States and Japan must be careful not to place undue expectations on ASEAN, noting that "we can't make ASEAN the frontline [of competition with China] given its weakness."[85] Another expert points out that any joint approach should be premised on "introducing change slowly across Southeast Asia with a focus on growing cooperation now so that it is hard [for China] to disrupt and is politically sustainable."[86] The way to do this, another expert contended, is through a mix of "empowerment and presence," combining joint training and building of partner capability together with cruising, port calls, exercises, and transits.[87]

Such points echo the findings of recent studies by leading U.S. scholars of Asia that suggest that competition is growing but that all is not lost so long as the United States and its allies respond thoughtfully. David Shambaugh, for example, says that "a subtle but noticeable

---

[80] Ministry of Defense of Japan, 2018.

[81] Jing Sun, *Japan and China as Charm Rivals: Soft Power in Regional Diplomacy*, Ann Arbor, Mich.: University of Michigan Press, 2012.

[82] Author interview with Japanese think-tank expert, Tokyo, April 2019.

[83] Author interview with Japanese government official, Tokyo, April 2019.

[84] Author interview with Japanese government official, Tokyo, April 2019.

[85] Author interview with Japanese academic, Tokyo, April 2019.

[86] Author interview with Japanese government official, Tokyo, April 2019.

[87] Author interview with Japanese government official, Tokyo, April 2019.

gravitation toward China has been apparent across the region" since 2016, but the United States still has "comprehensive comparative strengths vis-à-vis China in Southeast Asia," provided it plays its hand well.[88] Similarly, Cronin et al., 2019, advises the United States to adopt a strategy premised on greater bilateral engagement in the realms of economics, security, and diplomacy and via the U.S. alliance with Japan, but also cautions that

> [g]iven that most Southeast Asian countries are focused on sustaining economic growth and that Beijing remains the No. 1 trading partner of ASEAN, American diplomacy will have to walk a fine line that recognizes the reality that Southeast Asia has emerged as a contested space without framing U.S. engagement with the region as entirely driven by concerns about China.[89]

Japan's Security Cooperation with Southeast Asia Militaries Has Grown Rapidly over the Past Decade

According to official government documents, Japan's defense policy has been undergoing an important evolution in recent years, shifting

> from traditional exchanges to deeper cooperation in a phased manner by appropriately combining various means including joint exercises and capacity building assistance, defense equipment and technology cooperation, and the development of institutional frameworks.[90]

Japan divides its defense engagement with Southeast Asian nations into bilateral contacts and multilateral activities. Japan conducts bilateral and multilateral security dialogues and exchanges, including exchanges between defense ministers and high-level officials, regular (working-level) consultations between defense officials, unit exchanges, professional military educational contacts, and research exchanges. Multilateral contacts include a wide variety of security dialogues sponsored by ASEAN, the Japanese Ministry of Defense, multinational defense authorities and private sector multilateral groupings, and multilateral exercises and seminars.[91] For Japan, the most important of these dialogues is the ASEAN-Japan Defense Ministers' Informal Meeting, which has been held every two years since 2014.

Tokyo's assistance to the ASEAN Humanitarian Assistance Center, located in Jakarta, Indonesia, is another point of contact between Japan and the region. The Japan-ASEAN Integration Fund assists ASEAN nations with developing their national readiness and response plans in the event of a natural disaster.

---

[88] David Shambaugh, "Can America Meet the China Challenge in Southeast Asia?" *East Asia Forum*, May 22, 2018.

[89] Cronin et al., 2019, p. 19.

[90] Ministry of Defense of Japan, 2018, p. 345.

[91] Ministry of Defense of Japan, 2018, p. 347.

Additionally, Japan has been a participant since 2006 in the Regional Cooperation Agreement on Combating Piracy and Armed Robbery Against Ships in Asia, sharing information and assisting Southeast Asian nations threatened by piracy.[92]

A decade later, in November 2016, then Japanese Minister of Defense Inada Tomomi proposed Japan's Vientiane Vision, a statement of "the priority areas of the future direction of ASEAN-wide defense cooperation" focused on

> (1) Consolidating the order based on the principles of international law; (2) Promoting maritime security; and (3) Coping with the increasingly diversifying and complex security issues.[93]

In addition to dialogues and exchanges, Japan also promotes capacity-building assistance and other practical multilateral security cooperation initiatives with Southeast Asian nations aimed at

> (1) [e]nabling recipient countries to contribute to improving the global security environment; (2) strengthening bilateral relationships with recipient countries; (3) strengthening the relationships with other donor countries such as the United States and Australia; and (4) promoting Japan's efforts to work proactively and independently to realize regional peace and stability and to gain trust in the MOD [Ministry of Defense]/SDF and Japan as a whole. Capacity building assistance initiatives also facilitate the improvement of SDF capabilities.[94]

Japan further breaks down its capacity-building assistance to Southeast Asia into areas, including HA/DR, peacekeeping operations, maritime security, international law training, lectures and practical training, human resources development, and technical assistance with challenges such as engineering.[95] Japan's defense capacity-building activities in the Indo-Pacific are presented in Figure 4.2.

---

[92] Regional Cooperation Agreement on Combating Piracy and Armed Robbery Against Ships in Asia, "About ReCAAP Information Sharing Center," webpage, undated.

[93] Ministry of Defense of Japan, 2018, p. 349.

[94] Ministry of Defense of Japan, 2018, p. 351.

[95] Ministry of Defense of Japan, 2018.

Figure 4.2. Japan's Capacity-Building Assistance Activities

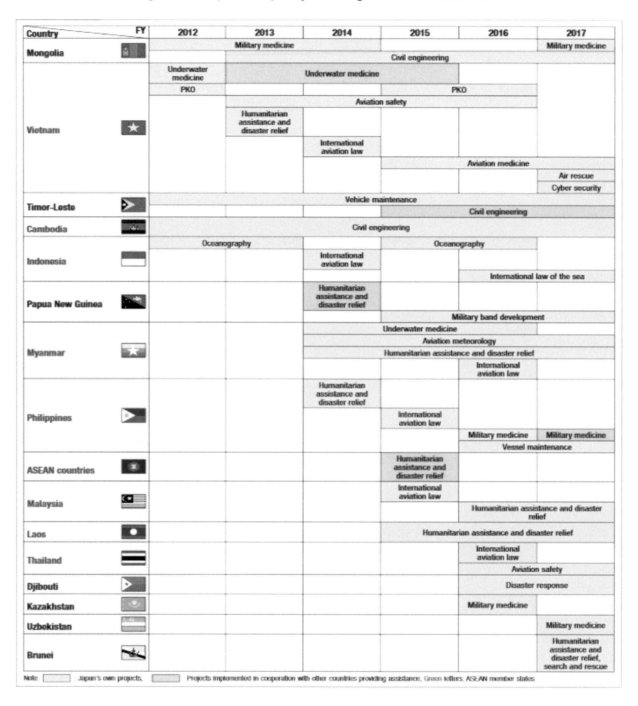

Country	FY	2012	2013	2014	2015	2016	2017
Mongolia		Military medicine					Military medicine
Vietnam			Civil engineering				
		Underwater medicine	Underwater medicine				
		PKO				PKO	
			Aviation safety				
			Humanitarian assistance and disaster relief				
				International aviation law			
						Aviation medicine	
							Air rescue
							Cyber security
Timor-Leste		Vehicle maintenance					
					Civil engineering		
Cambodia		Civil engineering					
Indonesia		Oceanography			Oceanography		
				International aviation law			
						International law of the sea	
Papua New Guinea				Humanitarian assistance and disaster relief			
Myanmar						Military band development	
				Underwater medicine			
				Aviation meteorology			
				Humanitarian assistance and disaster relief			
					International aviation law		
Philippines				Humanitarian assistance and disaster relief			
					International aviation law		
						Military medicine	Military medicine
						Vessel maintenance	
ASEAN countries					Humanitarian assistance and disaster relief		
Malaysia					International aviation law		
						Humanitarian assistance and disaster relief	
Laos					Humanitarian assistance and disaster relief		
Thailand					International aviation law		
					Aviation safety		
Djibouti					Disaster response		
Kazakhstan					Military medicine		
Uzbekistan							Military medicine
Brunei							Humanitarian assistance and disaster relief, search and rescue

Note: ☐ Japan's own projects, ▨ Projects implemented in cooperation with other countries providing assistance. Green letters: ASEAN member states

SOURCE: Ministry of Defense of Japan, 2018.

Country-by-Country Breakdown of Bilateral Defense Cooperation Ties

As written in the *Defense of Japan 2018*, "Japan and ASEAN member states have been working to foster trust and deepen mutual understanding through high-level and working-level exchanges and promoting effective cooperation such as capacity building cooperation, joint exercises, and defense equipment and technology cooperation."[96] This section includes a discussion of Japan's bilateral exchanges with each of the ten ASEAN member states, noting areas in which the JASDF has been active.[97] The following material is drawn from the *Defense of Japan 2018* in the order in which the countries are discussed in that document, and the descriptions in almost all cases flow from that document without further additions from the author.

Indonesia

Indonesia is important to Japan for its geostrategic location and regional diplomatic weight; it is also an archipelagic state and rising middle power that Tokyo hopes to deepen diplomatic, economic, and security cooperation with so as to better guard against regional threats. To that end, Japan in 2006 provided Indonesia with funds to procure three coastal patrol craft to counter piracy and better police its waters.[98] In December 2015, Japan and Indonesia held their first "2 + 2" foreign and defense ministers' meeting and agreed to commence negotiations on an agreement that would facilitate the transfer of further defense equipment and technology. In addition, the two sides participate in an Indonesia-hosted multilateral naval exercise (Exercise: Komodo), and Tokyo has supported Jakarta through capacity-building assistance in the realms of oceanography, international maritime law, and international aviation law.[99] In September 2017, the Abe administration announced it would help Indonesia develop radar stations on Weh Island (also known as Sambung Island) just west of Sumatra to monitor illegal fishing and promised to transfer radar to Jakarta for emplacement on the Natuna Islands, where China's self-proclaimed nine-dashed line overlaps with Indonesia's Exclusive Economic Zone.[100]

Vietnam

Vietnam has been a key focus for Japan's expanding external security cooperation, largely in the maritime domain, where Hanoi's resistance to Beijing's expansive South China Sea claims are seen by Tokyo as a useful obstacle to Chinese regional hegemony. In 2014, Japan and Vietnam agreed to elevate their overall relationship to an "Extensive Strategic Partnership"; four years later, the two sides signed a "Joint Vision on Japan-Vietnam Defense Cooperation" that serves as a guideline for future defense cooperation and exchanges. Defense ministers from the two sides have met regularly, including on the sidelines of multilateral meetings, such as the Shangri-La Dialogue, and a variety of exchanges (including on topics such as UN peacekeeping

---

[96] Ministry of Defense of Japan, 2018, p. 364.

[97] Materials in this section are largely drawn from the *Defense of Japan 2018*, with minor rewording for clarity and flow.

[98] Ministry of Foreign Affairs of Japan, *Japan's Official Development Assistance White Paper 2006*, Tokyo, 2006.

[99] Ministry of Defense of Japan, 2018.

[100] Kyodo News, "Japan Agrees to Help Develop Indonesia's Outer Islands, Promote Fisheries," *Japan Times*, September 7, 2017.

operations and capacity-building assistance) are ongoing. Japan has sought to support Vietnam in ensuring that the status of the South China Sea is resolved peacefully and without coercion and that the sea remains an open international waterway.[101]

The JMSDF has paid port calls at Cam Ranh Bay with destroyers in 2016, 2017, and 2018, and with submarines in 2018. In December 2017, a JASDF U-4 utility support aircraft flew to Da Nang while the Vietnamese Air Defense and Air Force Commander Le Huy Vinh visited Japan for talks with his JASDF service chief counterpart, leading to the establishment of a service-to-service relationship. Additionally, from mid-2017 onward, the JASDF has been engaged with Vietnam on programs to assist with air rescue, aviation medicine, and cybersecurity.[102]

Japan has also agreed to security-related cooperation in support of Vietnam's maritime law enforcement capabilities development, pledging six used coastal patrol craft in 2014 and six new boats in 2016, along with concessional loans to help offset the costs of the vessels.[103]

Singapore

Singapore is important to Japan as a regional partner of the United States that is actively invested in trying to preserve an open regional architecture with a rules-based order. In December 2009, Singapore became the first Southeast Asian nation to sign a memorandum of understanding on defense cooperation and exchanges with Japan, leading to 15 regular defense meetings that have included numerous reciprocal defense minister visits. In November 2017, a JASDF C-2 transport aircraft visited the Paya Lebar Air Base, and the JASDF service visited Singapore in early 2018 to attend the Singapore Air Show. JMSDF vessels have also made port calls, and other service-to-service exchanges have been held.[104]

The Philippines

Japan's defense ties with the Philippines include regular high-level exchanges, service-to-service contacts, naval visits, participation in multilateral exercises, and efforts to support capability development through the leasing and granting of defense equipment. Since 2016, Japan has transferred five JMSDF TC-90 training aircraft to the Philippines to enhance Manila's maritime domain awareness and ability to engage in HA/DR and airlift. Tokyo's assistance has extended to pilot training and maintenance for these platforms, as well as the granting of parts for used UH-1H utility helicopters.

The SDF and the Armed Forces of the Philippines have also engaged in periodic exercises focused on search and rescue, and Tokyo and Manila continue to discuss the possibility of a Status of Visiting Forces Agreement that would facilitate deeper contacts by enabling SDF

---

[101] Ministry of Defense of Japan, 2018.

[102] Ministry of Defense of Japan, 2018.

[103] Ankit Panda, "Japan Pledges 6 New Patrol Boats for Vietnam Coast Guard," *The Diplomat*, January 17, 2017.

[104] Ministry of Defense of Japan, 2018.

personnel to expand the types and locations of exercises they could undertake with their Filipino counterparts.[105] Additionally, after the 2017 siege of Marawi in the southern Philippines, Japan pledged grant aid of up to ¥2 billion (approximately US$18.5 million) to help with reconstruction of roads and other social infrastructure.[106]

Thailand

Japan's defense ties with the Kingdom of Thailand are long-standing, and Japanese interlocutors proudly point to the fact that former Commander in Chief of the Royal Thai Air Force Air Chief Marshall Johm Rungsawang is a graduate of Japan's National Defense Academy and Air Staff College.[107] Since the first Thai military officers were accepted in 1958, Thailand has sent the largest number of students to the academy.[108] Regular high-level defense exchanges are held, and Japanese forces have participated in the Thailand-hosted Cobra Gold exercise since 2005. An agreement on defense technology development and equipment transfer is under discussion but has yet to be finalized as of this writing.

In terms of service exchanges and contacts, JMSDF vessels visited Thailand in 2017, and a JASDF C-2 transport aircraft visited U-Tapao Royal Thai Naval Airfield in November of that year. In January 2018, a JASDF KC-767 refueling and transportation aircraft visited Don Mueang Air Force Base, and service exchanges were held. The JASDF has also engaged its Thai counterparts in seminars on aviation safety and international aviation law, and the Japan Ground Self-Defense Force (JGSDF) has hosted a seminar for the Royal Thai Army ahead of its deployment in support of the UN Mission in South Sudan.[109]

Cambodia

After assisting with the negotiations leading to the Cambodian peace process in the early 1990s, Cambodia was the first country Japan deployed forces to overseas after World War II, supporting the UN Transitional Authority in Cambodia in the early 1990s, which led to advances in Japan's legislation enabling UN peacekeeping operation activities. Tokyo's involvement in this process was well-received by Southeast Asian nations.[110] In December 2013, Tokyo and

---

[105] Manny Mogato, "Manila and Tokyo Need Tighter Security Ties," Rappler, February 13, 2019.

[106] Japan International Cooperation Agency, "Signing of the Grant Agreement with the Philippines: Contributing to the Stability and the Reconstruction of the Lives of the Victims in Conflict-Afflicted Marawi City in Mindanao Through Roads and Other Social Infrastructure," press release, May 16, 2018.

[107] Author interviews with Japanese government officials and think-tank experts, Tokyo, April 2019.

[108] Ministry of Defense of Japan, 2018.

[109] Ministry of Defense of Japan, 2018.

[110] Smith, 2019.

Phnom Penh agreed to upgrade their relationship to a "strategic partnership"; since that time, the JGSDF has trained the Royal Cambodian Armed Forces on road construction and engineering.[111]

Myanmar

Japan's defense exchanges with Myanmar date to that nation's democratic political transition in 2011 and have been fairly limited to date because of issues of absorptive capacity and distance. In addition to senior defense official exchanges, the JASDF has trained the Myanmar military, known as the Tatmadaw, on aviation meteorology, and the JGSDF has conducted seminars for its Burmese counterparts on HA/DR.[112]

Lao People's Democratic Republic

Japan's defense contacts with Laos have been growing from a low base since the Japanese defense attaché in Vietnam was appointed concurrently to manage ties with Laos in 2011. In March 2018, the first Lao students graduated from Japan's National Defense Academy, and the JGSDF has trained Lao People's Army engineering and medical officers on HA/DR.[113]

Malaysia

Tokyo's defense ties with Kuala Lumpur have been limited in recent decades, though the JGSDF arranged a seminar in November 2017 on HA/DR, and the two sides agreed to an arrangement in April 2018 that would facilitate the transfer of defense equipment and technology.[114]

Brunei

Defense exchanges at the level of defense minister have been held between Japan and Brunei Darussalam, and Japan has hosted capacity-building assistance programs and seminars on HA/DR and search and rescue.[115]

Conclusion

The descriptions above largely stem from published Japanese official documents. As the descriptions make clear, most of the focus Japan has put on regional defense cooperation has been in the arenas of exchanges, military medicine, engineering, and HA/DR; there has been relatively little focus on cooperation that would be directly related to air worthiness, safety, or combat operations because these remain sensitive for Japan. The next section advances the

---

[111] Ministry of Defense of Japan, 2018.

[112] Ministry of Defense of Japan, 2018.

[113] Ministry of Defense of Japan, 2018.

[114] Ministry of Defense of Japan, 2018.

[115] Ministry of Defense of Japan, 2018.

analysis by bringing in the perspectives of current and former Japanese officials, SDF officers, scholars, and think-tank analysts to provide additional perspectives and texture.

Japanese Experts' Views of U.S.-Japan Defense Cooperation to Compete with China in Southeast Asia

Interviewees for this study presented several interesting and thoughtful suggestions for how the United States and Japan might further expand and deepen their efforts to bolster Southeast Asian nations' autonomy, capacity, and resilience and, in so doing, improve their ability and willingness to resist Chinese pressure or coercion. One expert, for example, noted the desirability of expanding intelligence-sharing arrangements and increasing public diplomacy outreach. Expanded HA/DR programs, enhanced counterpiracy operations, and efforts to combat illegal, unreported, and unregulated fishing in the South China Sea could all be appealing to ASEAN states.[116] A second interviewee agreed with this approach, commenting that "the focus should be on helping Southeast Asian nations build up their coast guards and maritime law enforcement capabilities."[117] Capabilities such as radar can be useful for combating illegal, unreported, and unregulated fishing; piracy; arms trafficking and drug smuggling; and human trafficking but can also be used to create a common operational picture that improves coastal states' situational awareness in ways that could complicate China's ability to leverage its fishing fleet, maritime militia, and the China Coast Guard for gray zone coercion. Japan's assistance to Indonesia on radar tracking stations on Weh Island and in the Natuna Islands is a good example of this.

Japan is also focused on improving Southeast Asian nations' abilities to monitor their air and maritime spaces from the land, air, and sea and to understand their rights and other nations' responsibilities in these areas. Japan could also focus on training regional militaries in how to use, maintain, repair, and logistically support the hardware it or the United States transfers to Southeast Asia. As the sections above have detailed, Japan has been transferring used coastal patrol craft, maritime patrol airplanes, and radar to such countries as Indonesia, Malaysia, the Philippines, and Vietnam. When the JASDF phases out its use of the P3-C in three to five years, one interviewee argued, "this would be an ideal platform to transfer to the Philippines," noting that it is also important for Japan to balance the capabilities it transfers with "intellectual software" by continuing, for example, to "help to educate Southeast Asians about the history of China's activities in the region as well as various aspects of air transit laws."[118]

One possible focus of U.S.-Japan efforts to bolster ties with Southeast Asian nations could be the creation of a campaign to counter Chinese influence operations.[119] Another area that one

---

[116] Author interview with Japanese academic in Tokyo, April 2019.

[117] Author interview with Japanese think-tank analyst in Tokyo, April 2019.

[118] Author interview with Japanese military officer in Tokyo, April 2019.

[119] Author interview with Japanese academic in Tokyo, April 2019.

interviewee suggested would be an ASEAN-Japan joint exercise that might be "trilateralized" to include the United States.[120] In terms of defense exports and the transfer of excess defense articles and equipment, Japan is likely to focus on the sale or granting of "radar, small vessels, and communications systems," hardware that Japan has also sought to train recipient nations in how to use and maintain.[121]

In the event that China declares a South China Sea ADIZ, one interviewee asked,

> What would the U.S. want to see from Japan? Probably counter-patrols, escorts, efforts to sustain freedom of overflight, ISR, presence of airborne warning and control planes and fighters . . . Japan might be able to provide such things [but it would be complicated] . . . a multilateral response that included the United Kingdom, France and Australia in addition to the United States would help smooth the path for Japan to participate.[122]

"The key to defeating a South China Sea ADIZ," one interviewee said, "is to make ASEAN countries capable of air defense alert operations through the transfer of radar for air sovereignty."[123]

JASDF fighters in 2019 escorted U.S. Air Force B-52s in transits through China's self-proclaimed East China Sea ADIZ, something one interviewee noted when suggesting that such cooperation between the two nations' air forces could perhaps be extended to the South China Sea.[124] Although wartime cooperation might appear to be "a stretch at present," this interviewee pointed out that "peacetime and gray zone cooperation in the South China Sea has already begun," likely referring to Japan's decision over the past few years to begin sailing and training in the South China Sea and moving to bolster its ability to interoperate with the United States on naval aviation while building up regional partners' air and maritime domain awareness capabilities.[125]

Regarding Japan's efforts to build toward greater acceptance of Japanese military presence in the region and greater support inside Japan for such activities, interviewees stressed the importance of gradually introducing and expanding the areas, scale, and types of cooperation. They also generally noted that some of the more ambitious activities described below (1) would be controversial and possibly even extra-constitutional under prevailing interpretations of what Japan is permitted to engage in under the rubric of CSD, (2) would likely be seen as highly politically sensitive in Southeast Asia, (3) would certainly require a long period to build

---

[120] Author interview with Japanese military office in Tokyo, April 2019.

[121] Author interview with Japanese government official, Tokyo, April 2019.

[122] Author interview with Japanese government official, Tokyo, April 2019.

[123] Author interview with Japanese government official, Tokyo, April 2019.

[124] "B-52 Bombers Train with Japanese, US Fighter Jets over East China Sea," *Stars and Stripes*, March 21, 2019; author interview with Japanese government official, Tokyo, April 2019.

[125] Author interview with Japanese government official, Tokyo, April 2019.

acceptance, and (4) could still be impossible in the absence of a major disjuncture, such as a Chinese-initiated military conflict in the region.

Still, Japan's *Izumo*-class helicopter destroyer has routinely deployed around Southeast Asia every summer since 2017, making port calls in coastal nations and showing Japan's commitment to an open region. Additionally, Japan participates in the U.S. Navy's Pacific Partnership program on HA/DR and military medicine, most recently hosted in Vietnam (2018) and Singapore (2019). "HA/DR is a big opportunity—perhaps the biggest," one interviewee commented, adding that "our goal should be to introduce changes slowly across Southeast Asia, growing our regional cooperation now so that it's hard [for China] to stop [later] and becomes politically sustainable [with countries in the region]."[126]

Normalizing Japan's presence in the South China Sea and Southeast Asia region is something Japan has already started with its ASEAN-Japan Ship Rider Program, which brings officers from all ten Southeast Asian countries aboard Japan's helicopter destroyers for seminars on international maritime law, HA/DR, and networking.[127] In the air domain, Minister of Defense Iwaya Takeshi announced in October 2018 the establishment of the JASDF Professional Airmanship Program, which will invite officers from all ten ASEAN countries to observe JASDF training, participate in tabletop exercises, and engage in dialogue on HA/DR response.[128] One interviewee suggested that this program would highlight the international laws governing observance of and compliance with ADIZs and the rights of nations whose airframes are transiting ADIZs.[129]

An American official based in Japan agreed with this view, noting that "U.S.-Japan joint combat exercises in third countries could be possible if the U.S. pushes for it," adding that "some U.S. *gaiatsu* [pressure] might help facilitate" expanded Japanese defense activities overseas.[130] Another interviewee stated that if China tries to establish true control over the South China Sea, Japan might engage in "air escort of third country fishing or provide third countries with maritime domain awareness intelligence about Chinese Coast Guard operations or Chinese poaching activities."[131]

Another interlocutor was even more ambitious, suggesting that the United States and Japan should ultimately aim for a fully integrated defense posture that encompasses "both access to regional facilities and use of the region for power projection," suggesting that

---

[126] Author interview with Japanese government official, Tokyo, April 2019.

[127] Ministry of Defense of Japan, "Japan-ASEAN Ship Rider Cooperation Program: A Vientiane Vision Initiative," press release, June 19, 2017.

[128] "Japan Will Invite ASEAN Air Force Personnel to Observe ASDF Training: Iwaya," *Kyodo*, October 20, 2018.

[129] Author interview with Japanese think-tank expert, Tokyo, April 2019.

[130] Author interview, Tokyo, April 2019.

[131] Author interview with Japanese academic, Tokyo, April 2019.

[t]he U.S. and Japan should aim at integrated air and missile defense inside the first island chain. This would enable the U.S. Air Force to operate [close to China]. The Japan Air Self-Defense Force can sweep the areas between the first and second island chains. Over the long term, both Vietnam and the Philippines could be basing options for the USAF and the JASDF. This could be accomplished by first focusing on HA/DR, then expanding to joint training and exercises with third country partners, then moving to rotational deployments, and finally normalizing these to longer-term deployments.[132]

Presented with this idea, another interviewee responded positively, saying that

[i]f we need to gain access [to facilities in Southeast Asia] then we need to lay the groundwork [early]; access to such facilities does not have to be on a permanent basis. ISR is the starting point for cooperation with most Southeast Asian countries . . . that plus air domain awareness, radar, maintenance and repair, and meteorology and engineering [support].[133]

Yet another Japanese interviewee argued that the pathway to expanded joint U.S.-Japan access to facilities in Southeast Asia was to "begin with technology transfer and the training on operations and maintenance that goes along with that, then move on to military exercises with these countries, and finally to a possible discussion of [rotational access or] basing."[134] Access to a wider number of improved facilities across the Philippines would improve the prospects for "the U.S. and Japan to break China's South China Sea anti-access/area denial strategy," one observer argued, suggesting that, to pave the way for rotational access for JASDF assets, Japanese P3-C's could stop over in the Philippines en route to counterpiracy operations in the Gulf of Aden.[135] "The Philippines' lack of air domain awareness helps China and should be a source of concern for Japan and the U.S.," one interviewee said.[136]

Mindful of the position of regional air forces within their overall militaries and the politics of civil-military relations in Southeast Asia, one interlocutor cautioned that it is important to remember that "the air force is the last, and the least, of the services in importance for most Southeast Asian countries" and said that the United States and Japan, even as they prepare for possible military contingencies that might involve Southeast Asia, should remember that "connectivity is the key for the countries along the Mekong—with the exception of Vietnam, they are not particularly interested in defense and don't see it as very important."[137] But if Japan really wants a "reach" goal, one interlocutor commented, it might think about appealing to Southeast Asian nations by selling, transferring, or gifting some of its roughly 200 F-15 fighter

---

[132] Author interview with Japanese military officer, Tokyo, April 2019.

[133] Author interview with Japanese government official, Tokyo, April 2019.

[134] Author interview with Japanese government official, Tokyo, April 2019.

[135] Author interview with Japanese government official, Tokyo, April 2019.

[136] Author interview with Japanese government official, Tokyo, April 2019.

[137] Author interview with Japanese government official, Tokyo, April 2019.

fleet as that aircraft begins to be phased out in the coming years as Japan's F-35 fleet comes online.[138]

A final point that discussions with Japanese experts brought out came from outside of the Southeast Asia region in nearby Papua New Guinea, where Japan has helped establish and train that nation's first military band. As one specialist pointed out, "this is the first time that Japan has helped directly shape the existence and structure of the military of a foreign country," a development that could be relevant as the United States and Japan look to deepen their support for, and thereby improve the reception they receive in, Southeast Asia.[139] Although such a development clearly carries no operational implications, it was regarded by some Japanese interlocutors as a useful precedent that could later be turned to for more-substantial engagements with regional militaries.

Still, as one Japanese expert warned, it is important to bear in mind that Japan's primary focus is on applying its new legal modalities to expanded defense cooperation in Northeast Asia, closer to the Japanese home islands, rather than in Southeast Asia, saying that "some senior Japanese officials have stated that [the debate over the status of the] South China Sea is 'over.'"[140] Another Japanese expert agreed, arguing that expecting Japan to place a high degree of attention on building partner capacity in Southeast Asia would be a mistake, since Japan is not likely to dramatically increase its contributions in a short period, but a joint effort to "gradually" build up ASEAN's maritime domain awareness and ISR capabilities was more realistic.[141] It is worth remembering that challenges of politics, policy, resources, and legal and constitutional interpretations will also continue to constrain Japan's security cooperation with the region for some time.

Conclusion

In sum, Japanese interlocutors are pursuing a broad, step-by-step approach to build partner capacity in Southeast Asia—at times singly but sometimes jointly (where possible and acceptable to the partner nation)—in accordance with Japan's interests and alliance relationship with the United States. They can imagine ambitious goals and describe pathways and strategies by which to reach them but do not at present see such goals as likely, absent a long period of preparation and/or a major provocation by China that radically reorients the region's threat perceptions. A division of labor with the United States to cooperate in regard to dialogue, engagement, partnership-building, and strategy is something Japanese interlocutors see as

---

[138] Author interview with Japanese government official, Tokyo, April 2019.

[139] Author interview with Japanese think-tank expert, Tokyo, April 2019.

[140] Author interview with Japanese government official, Tokyo, April 2019.

[141] Author interview with Japanese government official, Tokyo, April 2019.

crucially important and is something the Japan Ministry of Defense is already pursuing to some extent.

In Chapter 5, the author provides some projections of where developments might go through 2030 and draws conclusions from the foregoing discussion.

5. Outlook and Policy Recommendations

This concluding chapter presents an overall assessment of the key factors that will shape the ability of the U.S.-Japan alliance to compete with China in Southeast Asia over the next five to ten years in the security and defense realms and presents a set of recommendations for U.S. defense and national security policymakers in general, as well as the USAF specifically.

Outlook for Regional Position and Partnerships Appears to Be Very Strong

Over the next five to ten years, the importance of the U.S. alliance to Japan is virtually impossible to overstate. Japan's defense engagement with China, by contrast, is virtually nonexistent and will likely remain so for the foreseeable future. With respect to Southeast Asia, Japan enjoys a largely positive overall image according to studies performed by Japan's Ministry of Foreign Affairs (Figure 5.1) and the ISEAS–Yusof Ishak Institute (Figure 5.2).

Figure 5.1. Japan's Regional Image in Southeast Asia

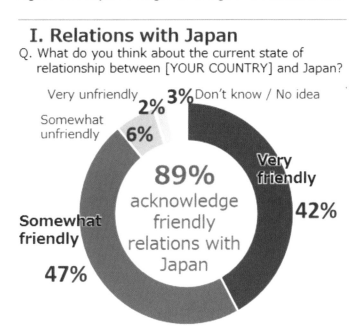

SOURCE: Ministry of Foreign Affairs of Japan, "Summary of the Results of an Opinion Poll on Japan in the Ten ASEAN Member States," November 1, 2017c.

Figure 5.2. Most Southeast Asians Surveyed Trust Japan to "Do the Right Thing" in Contributing to Global Peace, Security, Prosperity, and Governance

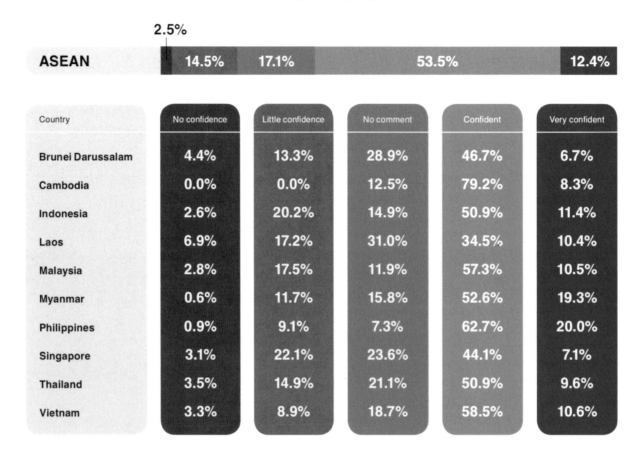

Country	No confidence	Little confidence	No comment	Confident	Very confident
ASEAN	14.5%	17.1%	53.5%		12.4%
Brunei Darussalam	4.4%	13.3%	28.9%	46.7%	6.7%
Cambodia	0.0%	0.0%	12.5%	79.2%	8.3%
Indonesia	2.6%	20.2%	14.9%	50.9%	11.4%
Laos	6.9%	17.2%	31.0%	34.5%	10.4%
Malaysia	2.8%	17.5%	11.9%	57.3%	10.5%
Myanmar	0.6%	11.7%	15.8%	52.6%	19.3%
Philippines	0.9%	9.1%	7.3%	62.7%	20.0%
Singapore	3.1%	22.1%	23.6%	44.1%	7.1%
Thailand	3.5%	14.9%	21.1%	50.9%	9.6%
Vietnam	3.3%	8.9%	18.7%	58.5%	10.6%

(ASEAN bar note: 2.5%)

SOURCE: Tang Siew Mun, Moe Thuzar, Hoang Thi Ha, Termsak Chalermpalanupap, Pham Thi Phuong Thao, and Anuthida Saelaow Qian, *The State of Southeast Asia: 2019 Survey Report*, Singapore: ISEAS–Yusof Ishak Institute, January 29, 2019, p. 29. Used with permission.

There is also a high degree of acceptance of the proposition that Japan should do more to engage with ASEAN nations, especially in Indonesia, the Philippines, and Vietnam (Figure 5.3).

Figure 5.3. Strong Support for Expanding Japan-ASEAN Security Cooperation

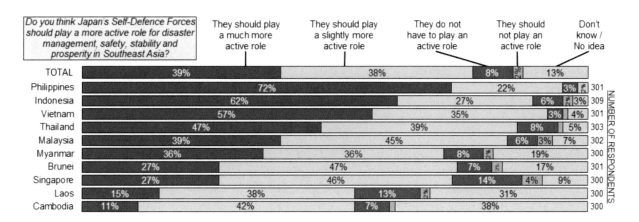

Do you think Japan's Self-Defence Forces should play a more active role for disaster management, safety, stability and prosperity in Southeast Asia?	They should play a much more active role	They should play a slightly more active role	They do not have to play an active role	They should not play an active role	Don't know / No idea	NUMBER OF RESPONDENTS
TOTAL	39%	38%	8%	2%	13%	
Philippines	72%	22%	3%	2%		301
Indonesia	62%	27%	6%	2% 3%		309
Vietnam	57%	35%	3%		4%	301
Thailand	47%	39%	8%		5%	303
Malaysia	39%	45%	6%	3%	7%	302
Myanmar	36%	36%	8%	2%	19%	300
Brunei	27%	47%	7%	2%	17%	301
Singapore	27%	46%	14%	4%	9%	300
Laos	15%	38%	13%	2%	31%	300
Cambodia	11%	42%	7%		38%	300

SOURCE: Ministry of Foreign Affairs of Japan, 2017b.

In light of China's growing power-projection capabilities, its emplacement of military facilities and hardware on the artificial islands it has built, and its aggressive use of its fishing fleet and other nonuniformed at-sea capabilities, it is not surprising that Southeast Asian nations are welcoming of Japan. U.S. and Japanese efforts to bolster the autonomy of ASEAN states, both individually and as a bloc, by providing them with diplomatic, legal, and other forms of support; assisting them in developing the capacity to monitor and police their waters and airspace; training them in operations and maintenance; assisting them through intelligence-sharing; selling or transferring them new or used defense and policing hardware; exercising with these nations; and working to bolster their resilience to and recovery from natural disasters will help focus on the values and interests that the United States, Japan, and ASEAN have in common.

Signposts that might indicate that the region is developing in a direction that is welcoming of more U.S.-Japan security and defense cooperation could include increases in tensions between China and key regional players, such as Indonesia, Malaysia, the Philippines, Singapore, and Vietnam, over competing territorial and/or maritime claims. By contrast, if China is able to manage its differences with these nations while continuing to woo such countries as Cambodia, Laos, Myanmar, and Thailand through arms sales, corruption, diplomatic protection in multilateral forums over human rights abuses, or investment, then the region might be less welcoming of the United States and less open to being wooed by Japan.

Options for the United States, Department of Defense, and U.S. Air Force

As U.S.-China competition deepens, the U.S.-Japan alliance is likely to play a critical role in overall U.S. defense strategy in the Indo-Pacific region. Tokyo welcomed the Obama administration's "pivot" or "rebalance" to Asia and has sought to support and promote the Trump administration's FOIP strategy while also seeking to synchronize its strategy with the

United States so as to achieve synergies in shared endeavors. Japan's desire to make proactive contributions to peace in coordination with its U.S. ally creates several policy opportunities for the United States and, specifically, for DoD and the USAF to consider.

Options for the United States

The U.S. government should consider strengthening defense and security cooperation with Japan in Southeast Asia as follows:

- *Understand that leveraging the U.S.-Japan alliance to compete with China in Southeast Asia requires "winning the peace," not trying to sell Southeast Asian nations on the need to gear up to fight a war with China.* Southeast Asian nations do not want to, and in all likelihood will not, fight China unless it is engaged in aggression against them directly. In the absence of such an unlikely event, most Southeast Asian nations will do little to nothing to counter China on behalf of other actors, including other Southeast Asian nations, Taiwan, Japan, or even the United States.[142] Additionally, constitutional, legal, policy, and political constraints on Japan, as well as defense policy priorities associated with the need to ensure sufficient resources for the defense of the home islands, would likely prevent Tokyo from undertaking much of a military commitment to any U.S.-China conflict in Southeast Asia. Therefore, it will be critical to ensure that competition with China over Southeast Asia remains peaceful and that countries in the region perceive the United States and Japan as doing everything possible to avoid an unwanted conflict by bolstering regional institutions, the rule of law, regional norms, and diplomacy. These efforts will place a premium on the use of the U.S. military and the Japanese SDF for peaceful, humanitarian missions rather than armed combat and suggest that military operations should be crafted so as to contribute to regional outcomes valued by ASEAN states, such as improving air and maritime domain awareness for military and law enforcement actors.
- *Jointly articulate a policy framework built around ASEAN centrality and the values of autonomy, capacity, and resiliency that Southeast Asians will find attractive.* The United States and Japan have both talked about FOIP. The United States has described FOIP as a "strategy," whereas Japan has increasingly shifted to talking about FOIP as a "vision" and has recently unofficially begun to describe its goal as a "free, open, and inclusive Indo-Pacific."[143] Southeast Asian nations, sensitive to being seen as a chessboard for great-power competition and leery of decisions being made that marginalize their autonomy or force them to choose between the United States or China, will respond better to U.S. and Japanese initiatives if they are framed in ways that emphasize respect for regional values and priorities. One of the foremost of these values is *ASEAN centrality*, or the notion that ASEAN is normatively the appropriate locus of Indo-Pacific integration and decisionmaking. ASEAN members will also respond better to initiatives that focus on enhancing their autonomy, capacity, and resilience and to partnering with

---

[142] Cronin et al., 2019; author interviews with Japanese government officials, academic specialists, and think-tank experts, Tokyo, April 2019.

[143] Author interviews with Japanese government officials, academic specialists, and think-tank experts, Tokyo, April 2019.

them to work on problems associated with economic development and security affairs while not signaling that such assistance is in any explicit way tied to an expectation that recipient states will either line up against China militarily or be forced to submit to being evaluated by outside actors for the degree of their democratic governance.[144]

Options for the Department of Defense and the United States Air Force

DoD and the USAF should consider the following options to deepen their relationships with Southeast Asian nations in tandem with Japan:

- *Frame U.S.-Japan security cooperation in Southeast Asia around assistance designed to deal with humanitarian disasters, transnational nonstate threats, and air and maritime sovereignty.* Many of the options for cooperating with Southeast Asia or strengthening Southeast Asian nations' security forces or militaries will be less provocative and more welcomed by the region if they are presented as intended for use in situations unrelated to China. Such an approach is also more likely to be palatable for Japan, which generally tends to focus on security (as opposed to defense or military) cooperation with foreign partners. For example, access arrangements and capabilities assistance designed to respond to natural or manmade disasters or to counter narcotics smuggling, human trafficking, terrorism, or piracy are all likely to be acceptable to Southeast Asian nations, even if some of these would also help prepare the region to better meet a security challenge or threat from China. For that reason, messaging from the U.S. Department of State and DoD and the Japanese Ministry of Foreign Affairs and Ministry of Defense (as well as the Ministry of Land, Infrastructure, and Transportation, which manages the Japan Coast Guard, and the Japan International Cooperation Agency, which distributes Japan's Official Development Assistance) should consider describing their assistance in ways that focus primarily on its value for meeting challenges other than the potential threat posed by Chinese aggression. At an appropriate time once such cooperation is established, such an approach could enhance the possibility for layering on additional access or rotational agreements or capabilities that would be relevant for China scenarios.
- *Ensure that security cooperation plans and programs to engage Southeast Asian nations and to aid and assist them are coordinated, deconflicted, and designed to achieve synergy with Japanese efforts.* This effort will require enhanced planning and information-sharing about U.S. institutional capacity-building efforts, defense exchanges, ship visits, arms sales and transfers of excess defense articles, transits, security assistance programs, and professional military educational exchanges so as to build something akin to a joint engagement plan with Japan for Southeast Asia. Such an approach could leverage areas in which Japan's diplomatic relations are stronger than U.S. ties are, while also ensuring that U.S. efforts are not duplicative of Japanese efforts but instead are synchronized to as great a degree as possible to build on each other's activities. Such an approach will undercut Chinese messaging that the United States is an illegitimate, extra-regional actor who should be ignored, while signaling to Southeast Asian nations that they can count on support from leading global actors in addition to the United States that seek to support their interests.

---

[144] Glosserman, 2019.

- *Where possible, consider engaging with Japan in planning and exercising HA/DR operations focused on responding to a crisis in Southeast Asia.* From the Indian Ocean tsunami of 2004 to Supertyphoon Yolanda, which hit the Philippines in 2013, the U.S. and Japanese militaries have repeatedly been in the lead on responding to the needs of vulnerable populations in Southeast Asia in the wake of catastrophic events. Coordinating the efforts of the two sides to preposition supplies, such as dry goods, potable water, medicine, fuel, and other relief necessities, and exercising the ability to deploy to key countries in the region in response to a disaster could help build trust-based personal relationships with key defense and civilian counterparts in these countries, as well as between the United States and Japan, and make access routine. HA/DR exercises, training, and preparation can help reduce losses of life and lay the foundation for deeper U.S.-Japan cooperation in other areas and can expand access for allies in Southeast Asia. Often, this will be a mission for fixed-wing air force assets that can rapidly deploy to devastated areas on short timelines and for rotary-wing platforms that can deliver aid to more-remote, damaged, or unimproved areas, followed by seaborne delivery of relief supplies en masse. It might even be possible, under certain circumstances, for U.S. and/or Japanese forces to assist foreign militaries with air mobility or air traffic control during a crisis, especially if it involves multiple nations and/or jurisdictions.

- *Consider expanding professional military education opportunities for Southeast Asian nations in the United States and Japan.* Early and mid-career professional military education can shape a foreign military's human capital and, in so doing, can affect its understanding of how best to organize, train, and equip to achieve operational effectiveness. Such security assistance programs can also build long-term positive relations between officers, who can climb the career ladder to positions of institutional leadership within foreign militaries. The U.S. experience with International Military Education and Training for Indonesia, the Philippines, and Thailand and Japan's experience with former Commander in Chief of the Royal Thai Air Force Air Chief Marshall Rungsawang attending a Japanese professional military education institution early in his career show that engagement with Southeast Asian militaries in the military education space should not be underestimated. The United States should encourage Japan to expand its professional military education opportunities for Southeast Asia and coordinate to target specific countries of interest to build allied engagement.

- *Explore opportunities to work with Japan to shape regional militaries through assistance programs focused on building partner capacity.* U.S. and Japanese efforts to assist Southeast Asian militaries with assessing the areas of weakness in their forces and acquiring additional military capabilities—most notably, radar, communications, and command and control systems and air and naval platforms (including maritime law enforcement and coastal patrol craft)—could be quite attractive to both Washington and Tokyo and, if pursued, should be done in a coordinated way. Key partners, such as Indonesia, Malaysia, the Philippines, and Vietnam, continue to have gaps in the capabilities needed to achieve air domain awareness and maritime domain awareness and to integrate and fuse their sensor data to produce a common operating picture that they could conceivably share with other regional actors to understand the situation in the South China Sea, for example. Indeed, Japan has already been assisting in the development of Vietnam's nascent space program, and this sort of capacity-building effort is one the United States might find worth partnering with to support.[145]

- *In engagements with Southeast Asian partners, leverage Japan's interest in and expertise with nonkinetic activities, such as logistics, maintenance, and training and exercises.* U.S. allies and partners in Southeast Asia have limited absorptive capacities for new hardware, and many of the benefits of transferring military capabilities to these countries will be lost if the recipient nations do not know how to support, maintain, repair, and effectively operate such platforms and systems. Japan has experience with less capable platforms and, because of budgetary constraints, has focused on extending the service life of military hardware through dedicated maintenance and repair, skills that Southeast Asian nations often have paid less attention to. U.S. military engagement with Southeast Asia could therefore prioritize this area in tandem with Japan and encourage partners to pay particular attention to this issue when working with the SDF.

- *Look for opportunities to trilateralize security cooperation with regional allies and partners in Southeast Asia so that they strengthen their institutional processes and improve their ability to operate with U.S. and Japanese forces.* U.S. efforts to engage Southeast Asian militaries exceed the efforts that Japan is engaged in, but where possible, routinizing Japanese presence and normalizing the allies' cooperation in Southeast Asia with third countries—especially other U.S. allies (such as the Philippines and Thailand) or close partners (such as Singapore)—would be valuable. Should a time ever come when the United States and Japan stand up a joint command, the allies will need to have laid the groundwork for access and overflight to employ truly interoperable and joint forces in a Southeast Asia contingency, and regular trilateral exercises with countries in the region could help pave the way for such an outcome. Moreover, Japan and the United States could work together on institutional capacity-building with third countries, particularly in the area of logistics (maintenance, sustainment, engineering). In some cases, however, a bilateral but complementary (and preferably coordinated) approach might be substantially more welcome by a given Southeast Asian state than joint U.S.-Japan security cooperation, which is more likely to carry political-diplomatic costs for the third nation's relations with China. In all cases, DoD and the Japanese Ministry of Defense should consult closely with their respective Department of State and Ministry of Foreign Affairs counterparts to understand what sorts of arrangements partner nations would be most open to and welcoming of.

- *Use information-sharing along with exchanges focused on the international laws and regulations governing air and maritime spaces to publicly highlight China's problematic behavior in the South China Sea and elsewhere, as well as the rights ASEAN states enjoy and their policy options.* U.S. and Japanese forces and officials could expand their efforts to engage Southeast Asian nations in information-sharing on Chinese activities in the South China Sea, providing situational awareness and supporting air and maritime sovereignty operations by regional actors, so that countries in the region understand what China is actually doing. At the same time, the United States and Japan should continue and, if possible, increase their training and legal exchanges with regional air and naval forces on issues of international law so that Southeast Asian nations understand their rights in these spaces. Finally, exchanges at the official, Track 1.5, and Track 2 levels

---

[145] Japan Aerospace Exploration Agency, "Vu Viet Phuong: A Successful Partnership," webpage, undated.

could be leveraged to help Southeast Asian nations understand how the United States and Japan are prepared to support them to help them understand their policy options.

Conclusion

The U.S.-Japan alliance is the cornerstone of U.S. force posture and presence and is a major factor enhancing U.S. influence and bolstering the appeal of liberal values and the international institutions that embody these values in the Indo-Pacific. The foregoing analysis has highlighted numerous ways that Japan, and the U.S.-Japan alliance, could be leveraged to compete with China in Southeast Asia. China, for its part, is not standing still, continuing to build out its network of investment and influence across the region. For the U.S.-Japan alliance, the time to move forward on a joint competitive strategy toward Southeast Asia that can nest within the FOIP strategy is now.

References

"Abe Shinzō Becomes Japan's Longest-Serving Prime Minister," Nippon Communications Foundation, November 20, 2019. As of April 6, 2020:
https://www.nippon.com/en/features/h00296/abe-shinzo-becomes-japan's-longest-serving-prime-minister.html

Agence France-Presse, "China Anti-Japan Protest Damage May Be over US$100M," *South China Morning Post*, November 13, 2012. As of January 20, 2020:
https://www.scmp.com/news/china/article/1081778/china-anti-japan-protest-damage-may-be-over-us100m

Armitage, Richard L., and Joseph P. Nye, *More Important Than Ever: Renewing the U.S.-Japan Alliance for the 21st Century*, Washington, D.C.: Center for Strategic and International Studies, October 2018.

"B-52 Bombers Train with Japanese, US Fighter Jets over East China Sea," *Stars and Stripes*, March 21, 2019. As of September 26, 2019:
https://www.stripes.com/news/pacific/b-52-bombers-train-with-japanese-us-fighter-jets-over-east-china-sea-1.573763

Bansho, Koichiro, "Japan's New Defense Strategy in the Southwest Islands and Development of Amphibious Operations Capabilities," in Scott W. Harold, Koichiro Bansho, Jeffrey W. Hornung, Koichi Isobe, and Richard L. Simcock II, *U.S-Japan Alliance Conference: Meeting the Challenge of Amphibious Operations*, Santa Monica, Calif.: RAND Corporation, CF-387-GOJ, 2018, pp. 8–15. As of April 6, 2020:
https://www.rand.org/pubs/conf_proceedings/CF387.html

Blackwill, Robert D., and Ashley J. Tellis, *Revising U.S. Grand Strategy Toward China*, Washington, D.C.: Council on Foreign Relations, Special Report No. 72, March 2015.

Blair, Dennis C., *Assertive Engagement: An Updated U.S.-Japan Strategy for China*, Washington, D.C.: Sasakawa Peace Foundation, 2016.

Blanchard, Ben, "Indian, Australian Warships Arrive in China for Naval Parade," Reuters, April 20, 2019. As of August 22, 2019:
https://www.reuters.com/article/us-china-military-anniversary/indian-australian-warships-arrive-in-china-for-naval-parade-idUSKCN1RX04W

Bush, Richard C., *The Perils of Proximity: China-Japan Security Relations*, Washington, D.C.: Brookings Institution Press, 2010.

Campbell, Kurt M., *The Pivot: The Future of American Statecraft in Asia*, New York: Twelve, 2016.

Chanlett-Avery, Emma, Liana W. Rosen, John W. Rollins, and Catherine A. Theohary, *North Korean Cyber Capabilities: In Brief*, Washington, D.C.: Congressional Research Service, R44912, August 3, 2017. As of April 6, 2020:
https://fas.org/sgp/crs/row/R44912.pdf

Cronin, Patrick M., Abigail Grace, Daniel Kliman, and Kristine Lee, *Contested Spaces: A Renewed Approach to Southeast Asia*, Washington, D.C.: Center for a New American Security, March 2019.

DoD—*See* U.S. Department of Defense.

"Editorial: To Be a Viable Force, CDP Must Show Grassroots Identity," *Asahi Shimbun*, October 4, 2018. As of September 26, 2019:
http://www.asahi.com/ajw/articles/AJ201810040022.html

Genron NPO, *Japan-China Public Opinion Survey 2018*, Tokyo, October 2018. As of September 26, 2019:
http://www.genron-npo.net/en/archives/181011.pdf

Glosserman, Brad, "FOIP Has a Problem with 'Free,'" Pacific Forum, PacNet No. 9, January 29, 2019.

Government of Japan, *National Defense Program Guidelines for FY 2011 and Beyond*, Tokyo, December 17, 2010.

———, *National Defense Program Guidelines for FY 2014 and Beyond*, Tokyo, December 17, 2013.

———, *Medium Term Defense Program (FY 2019-FY 2023)*, Tokyo, December 18, 2018a.

———, *National Defense Program Guidelines for FY 2019 and Beyond*, Tokyo, December 18, 2018b.

Green, Michael J., *By More Than Providence: Grand Strategy and American Power in the Asia Pacific Since 1783*, New York: Columbia University Press, 2017.

Green, Michael, and Jeffrey W. Hornung, "Ten Myths About Japan's Collective Self-Defense Change," *The Diplomat*, July 10, 2014. As of January 22, 2020:
https://thediplomat.com/2014/07/ten-myths-about-japans-collective-self-defense-change/

Ha, Matthew, and David Maxwell, *Kim Jong Un's "All-Purpose Sword": North Korean Cyber-Enabled Economic Warfare*, Washington, D.C.: Foundation for Defense of Democracies, October 2018. As of April 6, 2020:
https://www.fdd.org/wp-content/uploads/2018/09/REPORT_NorthKorea_CEEW.pdf

Harold, Scott W., Derek Grossman, Brian Harding, Jeffrey W. Hornung, Greg Poling, Jeffrey Smith, and Meagan L. Smith, *The Thickening Web of Asian Security Cooperation: Deepening Defense Ties Among U.S. Allies and Partners in the Indo-Pacific*, Santa Monica, Calif.: RAND Corporation, RR-3125-MCF, 2019. As of April 6, 2020: https://www.rand.org/pubs/research_reports/RR3125.html

Hornung, Jeffrey W., "Japan's Growing Hard Hedge Against China," *Asian Security*, Vol. 10, No. 2, 2014, pp. 97–122.

Hornung, Jeffrey W., and Mike M. Mochizuki, "Japan: Still an Exceptional U.S. Ally," *Washington Quarterly*, Vol. 39, No. 1, 2016, pp. 95–116.

House of Councillors, National Diet of Japan, "Strength of the Political Groups in the House of Councillors," webpage, undated. As of June 10, 2019: http://www.sangiin.go.jp/japanese/joho1/kousei/eng/strength/index.htm

House of Representatives, National Diet of Japan, "Strength of the In-House Groups in the House of Representatives," webpage, undated. As of June 10, 2019: http://www.shugiin.go.jp/internet/itdb_english.nsf/html/statics/english/strength.htm

Hsiao, Russell, "A Preliminary Survey of CCP Influence Operations in Japan," *China Brief*, Vol. 19, No. 12, June 26, 2019. As of January 20, 2020: https://jamestown.org/program/a-preliminary-survey-of-ccp-influence-operations-in-japan/

Human Rights Watch, *Human Rights in Southeast Asia: Briefing Materials for the ASEAN-Australia Summit*, Sydney, March 17–18, 2018. As of November 2, 2019: https://www.hrw.org/sites/default/files/supporting_resources/asean_australia0318.pdf

Hurst, Daniel, "Amid Thaw, Japan Is Seeing a Boom in Chinese Tourists," *The Diplomat*, March 27, 2019.

Jacobs, Jennifer, "Trump Muses Privately About Ending Postwar Japan Defense Pact," Bloomberg, June 24, 2019. As of August 22, 2019: https://www.bloomberg.com/news/articles/2019-06-25/trump-muses-privately-about-ending-postwar-japan-defense-pact

Japan Aerospace Exploration Agency, "Vu Viet Phuong: A Successful Partnership," webpage, undated. As of January 20, 2020: https://global.jaxa.jp/article/interview/2014/vol82/index_e.html

"Japan and China Agree on Security Hotline After a Decade of Talks," Reuters, May 9, 2018.

Japan External Trade Organization, "Japan's International Trade in Goods (Yearly): 2018," spreadsheet, 2019a. As of September 26, 2019: https://www.jetro.go.jp/en/reports/statistics.html

———, "Japan's Outward and Inward Foreign Direct Investment: FDI Stock (Based on International Investment Position, Net), 1996–2018: Outward," spreadsheet, 2019b. As of September 26, 2019:
https://www.jetro.go.jp/en/reports/statistics.html

Japan International Cooperation Agency, "Signing of the Grant Agreement with the Philippines: Contributing to Stability and the Reconstruction of the Lives of Victims in Conflict-Afflicted Marawi City in Mindanao Through Roads and Other Social Infrastructure," press release, May 16, 2018. As of September 26, 2019:
https://www.jica.go.jp/english/news/press/2018/180516_01.html

Japan Macro Advisors, "Cabinet Approval Rating," webpage, updated May 3, 2019. As of September 26, 2019:
https://www.japanmacroadvisors.com/page/category/politics/cabinet-approval-rating/

Japan National Tourism Organization (JNTO), "Japan Tourism Statistics: 2018 Breakdown by Country/Area," webpage, updated March 24, 2020. As of April 13, 2020:
https://statistics.jnto.go.jp/en/graph/#graph--breakdown--by--country

"Japan Will Invite ASEAN Air Force Personnel to Observe ASDF Training: Iwaya," *Kyodo*, October 20, 2018.

Jun, Jenny, Scott LaFoy, and Ethan Sohn, *North Korea's Cyber Operations: Strategy and Responses*, Washington, D.C.: Center for Strategic and International Studies, December 2015. As of April 6, 2020:
https://www.csis.org/analysis/north-korea's-cyber-operations

Kyodo News, "Japan Agrees to Help Develop Indonesia's Outer Islands, Promote Fisheries," *Japan Times*, September 7, 2017.

———, "Nippon Ishin no Kai Lawmaker Ousted from Party over Russia 'War' Gaffe," *Japan Times*, May 14, 2019.

Liff, Adam P., "Policy by Other Means: Collective Self-Defense and the Politics of Japan's Postwar Constitutional Reinterpretations," *Asia Policy*, No. 24, July 2017, pp. 139–172.

Liu Juntao, "Overseas Chinese and Chinese Soft Power from the Economic Perspective: The Case of Indonesia," *Science-Economy-Society* (科学经济社会), No. 3, December 2012, pp. 35–41.

Manicom, James, *Bridging Troubled Waters: China, Japan, and Maritime Order in the East China Sea*, Washington, D.C.: Georgetown University Press, 2014.

Ministry of Defense of Japan, *Defense of Japan 2016*, Tokyo, 2016a.

———, "Vientiane Vision: Japan's Defense Cooperation Initiative with ASEAN," Tokyo, 2016b.

———, "Japan-ASEAN Ship Rider Cooperation Program: A Vientiane Vision Initiative," press release, June 19, 2017. As of September 26, 2019:
https://www.mod.go.jp/e/press/release/2017/06/19b.html

———, *Defense of Japan 2018*, Tokyo, 2018.

———, *Defense of Japan 2019*, Tokyo, 2019.

Ministry of Foreign Affairs of Japan, "Trends in Chinese Government and Other Vessels in the Waters Surrounding the Senkaku Islands, and Japan's Response," webpage, undated. As of April 6, 2020:
https://www.mofa.go.jp/region/page23e_000021.html

———, *Japan's Official Development Assistance White Paper 2006*, Tokyo, 2006.

———, *The Guidelines for Japan-U.S. Defense Cooperation*, April 27, 2015.

———, *Diplomatic Bluebook 2017*, Tokyo, 2017a.

———, "Opinion Poll on Japan in Ten ASEAN Countries," press release, Tokyo, November 1, 2017b. As of September 26, 2019:
https://www.mofa.go.jp/press/release/press4e_001780.html

———, "Summary of the Results of an Opinion Poll on Japan in the Ten ASEAN Member States," November 1, 2017c. As of September 26, 2019:
https://www.mofa.go.jp/files/000304073.pdf

———, "Australia-India-Japan-U.S. Consultations on the Indo-Pacific," press release, Tokyo, November 12, 2017d.

Mogato, Manny, "Manila and Tokyo Need Tighter Security Ties," Rappler, February 13, 2019. As of April 6, 2020:
https://www.rappler.com/thought-leaders/223315-analysis-manila-tokyo-need-tighter-security-ties

Onodera Itsunori, "Strengthening Japan's Defense Force," *Asia-Pacific Review*, Vol. 20, No. 2, 2013, pp. 69–80.

"Over 100,000 Chinese Studying in Japan," Nippon Communications Foundation, May 8, 2018. As of September 26, 2019:
https://www.nippon.com/en/features/h00188/over-100-000-chinese-studying-in-japan.html

"Overseas Visitors to Japan in 2018 Top 31 Million," Nippon Communications Foundation, January 24, 2019. As of September 26, 2019:

https://www.nippon.com/en/japan-data/h00375/overseas-visitors-to-japan-in-2018-top-31-million.html

Panda, Ankit, "Japan Pledges 6 New Patrol Boats for Vietnam Coast Guard," *The Diplomat*, January 17, 2017.

Pew Research Center, "Global Indicators Database: Opinion of the United States: Japan," webpage, accessed January 20, 2020. As of January 20, 2020:
https://www.pewresearch.org/global/database/indicator/1/country/jp

"Red Revival: Communists Become Japan's Strongest Political Opposition in the Provinces," *The Economist*, April 17, 2015.

Regional Cooperation Agreement on Combating Piracy and Armed Robbery Against Ships in Asia, "About ReCAAP Information Sharing Center," webpage, undated. As of January 22, 2020:
http://www.recaap.org/about_ReCAAP-ISC

Reynolds, Isabel, "Japan, China Defense Ministers Meet for First Time in 3 Years," Bloomberg, October 19, 2018.

Schreiber, Mark, "Media Stews over Growing Chinese Numbers in Japan," *Japan Times*, July 14, 2018. As of September 26, 2019:
https://www.japantimes.co.jp/news/2018/07/14/national/media-national/media-stews-growing-chinese-numbers-japan/#.XQuv6sR7lPY

Seguchi, Kiyoyuki, "FDI Toward China: Japanese Companies Becoming More Aggressive," Canon Institute for Global Studies, March 11, 2019. As of January 20, 2020:
https://www.canon-igs.org/en/column/network/20190311_5631.html

Shambaugh, David, "Can America Meet the China Challenge in Southeast Asia?" *East Asia Forum*, May 22, 2018.

Smith, Sheila A., *Intimate Rivals: Japanese Domestic Politics and a Rising China*, New York: Columbia University Press, 2015.

———, *Japan Rearmed: The Politics of Military Power*, Cambridge, Mass.: Harvard University Press, 2019.

Sun, Jing, *Japan and China as Charm Rivals: Soft Power in Regional Diplomacy*, Ann Arbor, Mich.: University of Michigan Press, 2012.

Swaine, Michael D., Rachel M. Swanger, and Takashi Kawakami, *Japan and Ballistic Missile Defense*, Santa Monica, Calif.: RAND Corporation, MR-1374-CAPP, 2001. As of April 7, 2020:
https://www.rand.org/pubs/monograph_reports/MR1374.html

Tang Siew Mun, Moe Thuzar, Hoang Thi Ha, Termsak Chalermpalanupap, Pham Thi Phuong Thao, and Anuthida Saelaow Qian, *The State of Southeast Asia: 2019 Survey Report*, Singapore: ISEAS–Yusof Ishak Institute, January 29, 2019. As of April 30, 2020: https://www.iseas.edu.sg/images/pdf/TheStateofSEASurveyReport_2019.pdf

Terai, Shintaro, and Yusuke Matsuzaki, "Japan's 'China-Heavy' Companies Take Larger Hit to Profits," *Nikkei Asian Review*, February 8, 2019.

Tiezzi, Shannon, "China, Japan Close to Crisis Management Breakthrough," *The Diplomat*, March 4, 2015.

U.S. Department of Defense, "Joint Press Briefing by Secretary Mattis and Minister Inada, Tokyo Japan," transcript, February 4, 2017.

———, *Indo-Pacific Strategy Report: Preparedness, Partnerships, and Promoting a Networked Region*, Washington, D.C., June 1, 2019.

U.S. Department of State Office of the Spokesperson, "Advancing a Free and Open Indo-Pacific Region," November 18, 2018. As of November 2, 2019: https://www.state.gov/advancing-a-free-and-open-indo-pacific-region/

Wang Meiping, "Abe Speech to Indicate Japan's Future," *China Daily*, April 21, 2015.

Xu Mei, "The Driving Force and Restraining Factors of Southeast Asian Chinese in the Promotion of Chinese Soft Power," *Southeast Asian Studies* (东南亚研究), Vol. 6, 2010, pp. 58–65.

Yoshihara, Toshi, *Going Anti-Access at Sea: How Japan Can Turn the Tables on China*, Washington, D.C.: Center for a New American Security, September 2014. As of November 2, 2019: https://www.cnas.org/publications/reports/going-anti-access-at-sea-how-japan-can-turn-the-tables-on-china